Peadar O'Donnell

RADICAL IRISH LIVES

Series Editors: Maria Luddy and Fintan Lane

Other titles in the series

Louie Bennett by Rosemary Cullen Owens

Peadar O'Donnell

Donal Ó Drisceoil

CORK UNIVERSITY PRESS

First published in 2001 by
Cork University Press
University College
Cork
Ireland

British Library Cataloguing in Publication Data
A CIP catalogue record for this book is available from the British Library
ISBN 1 85918 310 7

Typeset by Tower Books, Ballincollig, Co. Cork
Printed by ColourBooks Ltd., Dublin

For Fionn,
and in memory of
Brendan and Seamus

But half-way down the drive we saw the writer
Still working in the garden with his wife.
I shouted and he straightened up to answer
And in the gloom his fine head glimmered white.

From 'Peadar O'Donnell' by John Hewitt,
The Bell, July 1942

Contents

Acknowledgements

Many people have helped, in a variety of ways, and I am indebted to them all: Fintan Lane, series joint editor, for inviting me on board and being a peerless fount of sources; Peter Hegarty, Peadar O'Donnell's most recent biographer, for his extraordinary generosity in sharing his research materials; Donal Donnelly, for the valuable materials and invaluable insights and memories; the wonderful Nora Harkin; Pat Maloney, the one-man library; Peadar Joe O'Donnell, Paddy Byrne, Val Mulkerns, D.R. O'Connor Lysaght, Anthony Coughlan and Jim Savage for agreeing to be interviewed or allowing interview material to be consulted; Geoff Roberts, who kindly copied Comintern material; Emmet O'Connor likewise; Benedict Kiely, Sheila McHugh, Tony Varley and Brian Hanley for giving access to unpublished papers; Robert MacNamara; Maurice Cronin; Kathleen Tucker; Eunan O'Halpin; John Horgan; Anton McCabe; Mary Ahern; Donnchadh Ó Corráin; Dave Edwards; Theresa Moriarty; May and James O'Donnell; Tony McGinley; all the good people at the Peadar O'Donnell Weekend in Dungloe and everyone at Cork University Press.

I am grateful, as always, to the staffs of the National Archives of Ireland; National Library of Ireland; Boole Library, UCC; Cork City Library; UCD Archives Department and the Irish Military Archives. Special thanks to Áine, Paul and family for their hospitality, Orla McDonnell for her patience and support, and, finally, Peadar O'Donnell, wherever he is, for the pleasure (and the pain!).

List of abbreviations

CPGB	Communist Party of Great Britain
CPI	Communist Party of Ireland
CPUSA	Communist Party of the USA
ECCI	Executive Committee of the Communist International
EPC	European Peasants' Committee
FSR	Friends of Soviet Russia
ICA	Irish Citizen Army
ILDL	Irish Labour Defence League
INTO	Irish National Teachers' Organisation
INUM	Irish National Unemployed Movement
IRA	Irish Republican Army
ITGWU	Irish Transport and General Workers' Union
IWFC	Irish Working Farmers' Committee
IWL	Irish Worker League
LAI	League Against Imperialism
NAUL	National Amalgamated Union of Labour
NISP	Northern Ireland Socialist Party
PCWRP	Preparatory Committee for the formation of a Workers' Revolutionary Party
RWG	Revolutionary Workers' Groups
SPI	Socialist Party of Ireland
WU	Workers' Union
WUI	Workers' Union of Ireland

Introduction

I do not think I have a gift for theoretical guidance. I see the world in terms of men and women and days and deeds, barriers, enemies, friends, with a sense of a tide underlying it all.

Gaelic American,
17 June 1939

The above quote forms part of one of Peadar O'Donnell's many denials throughout his life that he was a Communist. It is typical of the man: superficially self-deprecating, slightly vague and folksy, but fundamentally honest and politically committed. He was not a card-carrying Communist Party member, but from the late 1920s was increasingly a fellow-traveller of the 'official', i.e. Moscow-led, communist movement. His primary political involvement, however, was with the Irish republican movement, specifically the IRA. O'Donnell's mission, as he saw it, was not to graft communism onto republicanism, or transform the IRA from above; rather, it was to encourage the IRA in particular, and republicanism in general, to realize its true historical role by combining the struggles against capitalism and British imperialism. His relationship with the communist movement, at home and abroad, was closely related to that mission.

He was an activist and agitator, not a theoretician, and while he was a 'convinced Marxist' from an early stage, Marxist theory was 'a guide to action', not a dogma. 'Theory with me is the interpretation of the situation as it bursts in my face', he once wrote; 'that is why my views have been developed in a series of yelps.'[1] He has been described as 'the greatest agitator of his generation'[2] and, with the exception of Jim

1

Larkin, it is difficult to think of anyone to match him in Ireland in the first half of the twentieth century. The 'tide' he refers to is Marxist determinism, and he never doubted (despite the apparent accumulation of evidence to the contrary throughout his long life) that the course of history was ultimately, and inevitably, on his side. Here lay the basis of his legendary optimism: 'People talk of my optimism. I'm not optimistic in any bizarre sense. I believe in the historical process.'[3] James Connolly was clearly his main theoretical inspiration, and O'Donnell placed him in pride of place in a pantheon of influences that included Wolfe Tone, Fintan Lalor, Liam Mellows, David Fitzgerald, George Gilmore and Sean Murray. All were linked, for O'Donnell, by their part in the Irish revolutionary tradition, and by their efforts to identify, articulate and/or activate its social revolutionary dimension (which for him was its essence) at various stages of Irish history.

Peadar O'Donnell's importance as a radical figure is biographical rather than theoretical. In other words, it was what he did and tried to do during the historical period in which he was most active, rather than any body of political or theoretical writings that he left behind, that makes him significant. His deeds, of course, included writing seven novels, a play, three autobiographical accounts, several pamphlets and many thousands of words of campaigning journalism, but he never saw his writing, including his fiction, as distinct from his politics, just as he never distinguished between his socialism and republicanism. His novels were socialist narratives, stories of struggle. Referring to his literary output, he told his publishers: 'My pen is just a weapon and I use it now and then to gather into words scenes that surround certain conflicts.'[4] This being a political biography, O'Donnell's literature is viewed primarily in relation to its political dimension: the context in which it was written and the political messages contained within it, sometimes subtle, sometimes not. This is the fourth biographical treatment of Peadar O'Donnell, but the first to attempt to treat his politics in a chronological, systematic way.[5]

The formative period of O'Donnell's politics was 1918–21, when the energies and hopes of Irish republicanism and international communism co-existed. The attempt to synergize what he saw as these complementary political movements became, in many ways, his political life's work. He persevered with his arguments within a republican movement that remained largely resistant, and in his search for allies fell increasingly under the thrall of an international communist movement that had effectively become a policy instrument of Stalin and the Soviet Union. Once

Irish republicanism developed in directions that left his own vision isolated – into the populist reformism of Fianna Fáil and the apolitical militarism of the IRA – his politics became progressively closer to those of the Irish orthodox communist movement. However, to see Peadar O'Donnell only in the context of republicanism and communism offers too narrow a perspective. He had a stubborn individualism and impish contrariness that constantly defied efforts to compartmentalize him. While he regarded his cultural work and his agitational and organizational efforts on behalf of workers, small farmers and emigrants as part of the overarching socialist republican project, it is also possible to regard his activities in these areas separately – to acknowledge the multiple dynamics at work and catch glimpses of aspects of Irish history, at home and abroad, that lie outside an end-oriented, state-centred interpretative framework. O'Donnell, a traditional Marxist, never conceptualized his activism in such a way, but it can offer us another perspective, and counterbalances his own conclusion that he was 'never on the winning side in any damn thing ever I did'.[6]

Peadar O'Donnell lived from 1893 until 1986 and was a political animal for most his life: from his childhood and youth – influenced by a radical and progressive mother, the community spirit that sustained his people in the face of impoverishment, and the growth of the radical movements of co-operativism, trade unionism and separatist nationalism; through his most politically and creatively active period from his mid-twenties to his early forties, when he was carried by events from trade unionism into the IRA, which he tried unsuccessfully to reorient in a social revolutionary direction while writing fiction with the purpose of fomenting rebellion; to the second half of his life when, as the 'grand old man' of the Irish left, he accepted that reform and progressive change were all that could be achieved until, 'somewhere out the road in history',[7] the revolution would eventually and inevitably come. In a short book such as this, it is difficult to do full justice to such an eventful and extraordinary political life. However, the writer Benedict Kiely recalled that 'as author and editor Peadar O'Donnell always believed that there was nothing that could not gain by cutting and condensation',[8] and I present this work in the hope that he was right.

1

'Let us become rebels'
1893–1921

In the late nineteenth century the townland of Meenmore, near Dungloe in the Rosses of west Donegal, was a 'quiltwork of small fields' running down to the Atlantic, dotted with about fifty thatched cottages. It was here that Peadar O'Donnell was born in February 1893.[1] His mother Brigid (Biddy) and father James Sheáin Mór ran a typical five-acre holding, growing oats and potatoes, cutting turf in the surrounding bogs and fishing 'for the pot' in Dungloe Bay. His parents additionally supported themselves and their nine children (six boys and three girls – four other children died in infancy) in the standard manner for their class in the area at this time: James took part in the annual summer exodus of men, boys and single women to Scotland to pick potatoes ('tatie hoking'), while Biddy knitted socks as a low-paid outworker for the clothing industry. Just as in the rest of post-Famine rural Ireland, permanent emigration was intrinsic to the socio-economic structure in west Donegal, with Scotland being a staging post on the way to America, where the majority of the O'Donnell children eventually settled. James was unusual in having waged winter work in the local oat mill, a crucial factor in sparing his children the hardship endured by many of their peers, of being hired out as virtual slave labourers to larger farmers to the east at the notorious hiring fares, a fate described so memorably by the Donegal writer Patrick MacGill in *Children of the Dead End* (1914). Peadar's eldest brother John was the only one to have been hired out (for six months), though he and most of the others (not Peadar) joined their father at the gruelling work of tatie hoking once they reached their early teens. The sowing and saving of potatoes, turf cutting and many other common activities were performed by 'gatherings' or communal work groups, and the pattern of community solidarity or neighbourliness is the dominant motif in O'Donnell's reminiscences and literature; within it he identified the raw materials of a future socialist society.

The O'Donnell house was a standard two-roomed thatched cottage, but the household was unusual in being a hub of music and learning. James Sheáin Mór was an accomplished fiddler who played at dances and gatherings in their own house, on 'the green' outside and throughout the Rosses. Their home was also a 'reading-house' where his parents read and wrote letters for illiterate neighbours and kept a large stock of books, including most of the classics, which were devoured by the young Peadar (or Peter, as he was christened; he Gaelicized his name in 1918).[2] He described his mother as 'an advanced thinker' who set great store by education. Peadar began school early, around the time of his third birthday; however, as he suggested himself, this had as much to do with his mother getting him out from under her feet in the crowded cottage as wanting the bright youngster to get an early start. He liked school and became a star pupil, perhaps even a 'pet', his teachers ensuring his prominence during the visits of the inspectors. He won an essay competition in the local newspaper on his ambition to become a religious missionary; as he said later, however, a vocation could not be supported on a couple of acres of bogland. His rebellious instincts were in evidence at an early age: his teacher's fear of exposing the inspector to 'seditious ideas' saw him censor an essay of O'Donnell's on the local St Patrick's Day parade in which he regretted the absence of banners in defiance of British rule in Ireland. On another occasion he got 'a belt in the gob' for his 'cheeky' support of the co-operative movement, which came to his area in his last year at primary school.[3]

The movement arrived in the shape of the Templecrone Co-operative Agricultural Society, established in 1906 by Paddy 'The Cope' Gallagher, a local man who had gained experience of co-operatives in Scotland. The co-op (or 'cope', as it was known) was a direct challenge to the power of the 'gombeens', merchants whose power was based on their additional roles as moneylenders and buyers of local produce. The gombeens supported by the clergy, led the opposition to the co-op, and the issue caused division and rancour in the community. O'Donnell's mother was a supporter of the co-op and the first public meeting he ever attended was one addressed by Rev T.A. Finlay, a prominent advocate of co-operativism. Finlay had to face down rumours that he was not a priest at all, but a 'blackguard' dressed in stolen priest's clothes who was 'gadding around' with a 'widow woman' from America. The young Peadar squirmed when he saw Finlay's tobacco-stained teeth, antici- pating the opposition's claims that this was evidence of his non-clerical status! Despite the intense opposition, the co-op thrived and expanded, becoming the third largest agricultural society in the country by 1917.[4] While welcoming its success, O'Donnell later regretted the limitations of the initiative, and of Gallagher himself, who opposed attempts by co-op workers to unionize and was hostile to the independence struggle. Peadar's brother Frank was among those who had unsuccessfully attempted to unionize the workers and he left his job in the co-op store when Gallagher opposed his membership of the Irish Volunteers.[5]

While most of his contemporaries left school (if they attended at all) once they had reached the ages of nine to eleven, O'Donnell was fortu- nate that his mother encouraged and enabled him to stay on until he was fourteen. 'I wouldn't say I was better than many others', he told an interviewer. 'Fellows like Paddy John Jack and Eddie Jamie Charlie were much brighter, but I was lucky.'[6] In 1907 he secured the post of 'monitor', a type of teacher's assistant or apprentice, which allowed him to continue his education, at Roshine national school near Burtonport. He served four years there, and was also posted briefly to the island of Inniskeeragh, the setting for his second novel, *Islanders* (1927).[7] Encour- aged by his maternal aunt Madge, a teacher, the eighteen-year-old successfully sat the King's Scholarship examinations in Derry in 1911 to gain access to teacher training college in Dublin, and headed to Scotland for the summer to earn money for the year ahead. However, his plans for potato picking in Linlithgow were scuppered by a strike and he and his eldest brother John made their way to Glasgow and the rough world of the 'models' – lodging houses populated mainly by Irish migrants, described by O'Donnell as 'stepped up, tramp doss-houses: and not too much stepped up'. He drifted around Glasgow, often hungry, observing the hard life of the Irish migrants, whose cause became a life-long concern, until he was eventually seen safely onto the Derry boat by John.[8] The world of the migrant Irish worker has been captured bril- liantly in the literature of Donegal's 'navvy poet', Patrick MacGill, a committed socialist whose writings were an early influence on O'Don- nell. MacGill's autobiographical novels, *Children of the Dead End* and *The Rat Pit*, were published in 1914 and 1915 respectively, to commercial and critical success in England and resentment and hostility in Ireland, particularly from the powerful clergy who objected to MacGill's portrayal of priests. O'Donnell's mother, Biddy, characteristically, was one of the few to take MacGill's side.[9]

In September 1911 O'Donnell began his two-year teacher-training course at St Patrick's College in Drumcondra, run by the Catholic Vincentian order. These were not particularly happy years. The trainees endured strict curfews, poor food, an understocked library and dull courses. Student life was 'pretty arid' politically, and O'Donnell had not yet developed a sufficient interest in politics to be more than a detached observer when he twice saw James Connolly being heckled at street meetings. These pre-First World War years were turbulent and dynamic on the political and industrial fronts. James Connolly, Ireland's foremost socialist thinker, was at this time an organizer for the Irish Transport and General Workers' Union (ITGWU), founded in late 1908 by Jim Larkin, who came to personify the wave of industrial action ('Larkinism') that swept Ireland from 1907. This radical movement provoked increasingly militant responses from employers, culminating in the five-month 1913 lockout in Dublin. The lockout ended in victory for the employers and the state, and massive defeat for the new Irish labour movement. That defeat, coupled with the support of Irish people and the international socialist movement for the First World War, helped to drive James Connolly towards his fatal involvement in the separatist Easter Rising of 1916, an involvement that was crucial in the legacy it left to Irish socialists.

Although west Donegal was far from the storm centre in those turbulent years, O'Donnell remembered 'more talk of Larkin at home than in college' as his mother was a 'fervent Larkinite' and an 'evangelist' for his cause.[10] Her sister Madge, an activist with the Irish National Teachers' Organisation (INTO) was similarly disposed, as was their brother Peter, a member of the syndicalist Industrial Workers of the World ('Wobblies') in Butte, Montana, who returned to Donegal in 1913.[11] His mother and her family left their mark politically on O'Donnell, imbuing him with a class consciousness and syndicalist sensibility that would bear fruit in a brief but brilliant career as a trade unionist during the early stages of the next wave of union militancy that ran from 1917 to 1923.

Teaching and the INTO

Having survived St Patrick's and completed his training, the twenty-year-old O'Donnell returned to the Rosses in the summer of 1913 to take up his first teaching post on Innisfree island, a mile out to sea from his home in Meenmore. In 1915 he secured the headship of the two-teacher school at Derryhenny on the mainland, nine miles from Dungloe. The Derryhenny schoolhouse was 'a hovel' and in filling out his annual returns he left the authorities in no doubt as to its state of disrepair: 'How often was the school floor washed during the year? – Every time it rained heavily . . . Is there a school museum? – No, but the school should be in a museum', and so on. He wrote to the Education Office requesting an umbrella for use in school during heavy showers, and one night in early 1916 proceeded to demolish the dilapidated building with the help of some friends, forcing the authorities to fund the construction of a new one.[12] The good humour and creative direct action that would characterize his later political agitation were in evidence here, while his last entry in the Derryhenny day-book hinted at his literary inclinations: 'This ends the first chapter of my life. I wonder when autumn comes will it bring those lovely things that spring has promised.'[13]

He began to write on Arranmore Island, where he took over as headmaster of the Number One National School in July 1916. Arranmore was a large island adjacent to Innisfree where 300 families supported two schools and nine teachers at the time of his arrival. He set aside an hour a day for writing and seems to have been considering a future in journalism. Although an enthusiastic and innovative teacher, he found the job static and began to develop a distaste for it.[14] His period in Arranmore also saw the beginnings of his trade union activism and the first hints of a radical public persona that would subsequently become one of the best known in Ireland. O'Donnell's union was the INTO, which, along with the rest of the union movement, underwent a period of radicalization in the post-1916 period. There was an upsurge in union membership and activity related to wartime inflation, inequity in the hardships endured and increased demand for labour. The ITGWU revived and expanded rapidly, in conjunction with the militant separatist movement, which organized under the umbrella of Sinn Féin. O'Donnell was elected Donegal INTO county secretary in July 1917 and over the next year became, according to a contemporary account, 'the leading spirit' of the union in the county.[15] He campaigned on a number of issues, including education policies and funding as well as teachers' pay and conditions. Although O'Donnell himself, in distant retrospect, dated the beginnings of his political (socialist) education, including his introduction to the writings of Connolly, to his arrival in Liberty Hall in the second half of 1918, Anton McCabe has shown that at least a year earlier he was revealing an acquaintance with the ideas of Connolly and displaying the outline of a revolutionary socialist world-view. In a letter to the *Derry Journal* in November 1917, he wrote: 'What we want in Ireland is that our politics be discussed from the social and economic point of view.'[16] Addressing a Letterkenny teachers' meeting in the following February, he delivered these fiery revolutionary words:

> Let us see that no revolutionary party, who is goaded by economic hardship or inspired by honest interest in the onward march of labour, lacks the full sympathy of Irish teachers. Let us convert our schools into hotbeds, where working men's interests are fostered. Let us fling ourselves among the most fervent of social and economic revolutionists. Let us enlist the Labour world in our struggle with our tyrannical masters. If that means that the teachers of Ireland must become rebels, because their employers happen to be the state, then, in God's name, let us become rebels.[17]

The INTO affiliated to the Irish Labour Party and Trade Union Congress (ILPTUC) in 1918 and in March of that year O'Donnell oversaw the affiliation of his Gweedore and Rosses branch of the union to the Derry Trades Council, which he attended as a delegate from June. In that month also he expanded his activities into the wider labour movement, a move that, by end of that summer, would lead to his leaving teaching to become a full-time union official.

Trade unionist

From the late nineteenth century the work on the Scottish potato harvest was dominated by tatie hokers from Ireland, principally from west Donegal and west Mayo. O'Donnell's home in early 1918, Arranmore, along with his later home, Achill Island in Mayo, were particularly dependent on this annual work. The Scottish potato merchants organized work for the hokers, who were housed by the farmers in bothies, a generic term for a variety of outhouses, barns, byres, store houses and lofts. Conditions and pay were poor and in 1918 the Irish and Scottish labour movements combined in efforts to organize these exploited seasonal workers. In April of that year attempts were made to establish a Migratory Workers' Union, affiliated to the British-based National Amalgamated Union of Labour (NAUL), which was strong among unskilled workers in Derry and east Donegal. In June 1918 O'Donnell chaired a meeting to establish the Arranmore Migratory Labourers' Union, but it was the ITGWU, expanding rapidly from early 1918, which emerged as the dominant force as tatie hokers, mostly from Arranmore and Achill islands, joined in significant numbers. Meetings were held and demands on pay and conditions drawn up. The Scottish Potato Merchants' Association was informed that the labourers would not be travelling to Scotland that year unless their demands were met. A train was sent by the merchants to bring the workers to the boats but nobody boarded. The merchants were forced to negotiate with the ITGWU, which sent representatives to Scotland. O'Donnell also travelled and was involved, through his role on the the Derry Trades Council, in enlisting the help of the Glasgow Trades Council, a militant body which contained such notable British labour leaders as Manny Shinwell and Willie Gallacher. Joe Duncan of the Scottish Farm Servants' Union was also involved and it was eventually agreed that the tatie hokers' dispute would be settled by arbitration by the Ministry of Labour. It appears that the outcome was some slight improvements in pay, but conditions of living and work remained largely unchanged.[18] Subsequently, the tatie hokers were organized by Joe Duncan in the Scottish Farm Servants' Union, which retained its contact with the ITGWU and two years later a more successful strike was held, with O'Donnell at the centre of co-operation between the two unions.[19]

He spent time with the tatie hokers who had arrived late to Scotland in that summer of 1918, staying in a bothy on a farm in Ayrshire. But it was the three or four days O'Donnell spent in Glasgow, site of the legendary Red Clydeside, and his contact with socialist labour leaders, like Gallacher (later a Communist MP and who had been involved in the wartime shop steward and strike movement), that were really significant. His discussions there opened him up 'to the exciting world . . . of the working class struggle' and copperfastened in his mind 'the idea of working class agitation and the complete change of society'.[20] He initially enquired about the possibility of work within the Scottish labour movement, but Willie Gallacher encouraged him to return to Ireland and play his part in the expanding Transport Union. O'Donnell wrote to Liberty Hall, the headquarters of the ITGWU, asking if there was a place for him as an organizer. His INTO activities had made him known to Liberty Hall and the union was delighted to take him on, particularly as it was weak in Ulster.[21] This weakness arose from the strength of the British-based (amalgamated) unions such as the NAUL and the Workers' Union in the province, and the suspicion of many Protestant/Unionist workers that the ITGWU was an Irish nationalist organization. Important, if temporary, inroads were soon made as

O'Donnell came into his own, combining determination with flair as a roving organizer. In the words of the union's paper, he 'blazed a trail of glory clean across Ulster'.[22]

Peadar O'Donnell became a full-time trade unionist at a defining moment in Irish labour and political history, and it was a formative period in his life. The attempted imposition of conscription on Ireland in early 1918 had transformed the political scene. The labour movement participated in the general nationalist resistance to conscription, but crucially allowed the bourgeois nationalists of Sinn Féin to take the lead, establishing the pattern of the following years. Strikes were held against conscription and British militarism, but the labour leadership ensured that they occurred within the integrationist nationalist consensus. The Connollyite notion of the centrality of working-class revolution to the cause of national liberation was shelved and replaced by the idea that 'Labour must wait' until the pan-class national revolution had run its course. Labour withdrew from the December 1918 election which followed the end of the First World War. Sinn Féin won a substantial majority, and in January 1919 established Dáil Éireann as an independent Irish parliament in defiance of British rule.

At the time of O'Donnell's arrival there in the autumn of 1918, Liberty Hall was headquarters not only of the ITGWU, but of two organizations that had been associated with James Connolly and revived after 1916: the Socialist Party of Ireland (SPI) and the Irish Citizen Army (ICA). Both of these groups, and individuals within them, were influential on the young trade unionist. The SPI had been revived in 1917 by two of the leading figures in the ITGWU, William O'Brien and Cathal O'Shannon. It organized events such as a 10,000-strong demonstration in Dublin in October 1917 in celebration of the Bolshevik revolution, but its main focus was educational and propagandist; its leaders were also members of the Labour Party and appear to have used the SPI to maintain a radical image. The party had its base, including a library, in Liberty Hall and O'Donnell joined up, sponsored by Seamus Hughes, an ITGWU official who was also a member of the Irish Republican Brotherhood (IRB). Attending lectures and discussions, he was appalled by his own ignorance. Hughes gave him a copy of Connolly's *Socialism Made Easy* and he proceeded to read everything else in the library. It was on a trip to Ballina that he was introduced to *Das Kapital*, which he 'devoured', becoming, as he put it himself, 'a very convinced Marxist'. A plumber in that town gave O'Donnell ('flushed with my new found Socialism') the 'best advice of my life. . . . He advised me to talk to people in terms of their own experiences.' It was advice that he took to heart and it is evident in much of his future political activity.[23]

At Liberty Hall in the summer and early autumn of 1918, O'Donnell was associated with a small group of left-wing trade unionists led by Archie Heron, and was also influenced by Citizen Army veterans like Bob de Coeur. The ICA had originally been formed as a defence force for workers against police attacks in 1913, but under Connolly's guidance had broadened its remit to become an army fighting for a workers' republic. Following the death of Connolly and the defeat of the 1916 Rising, in which it took part, the ICA was never again a significant force. Though it retained an autonomous structure and an emotional appeal, and had rebuilt its membership to 200, relations were poor with the ITGWU leadership and rather than develop autonomously as a revolutionary force, it ended up as a mere appendage of the IRA in the upcoming war of independence and civil war. O'Donnell was disappointed that he was not encouraged to join the ICA and that it did not seem to have a place within the union. Yet he was convinced by his associates in Liberty Hall, and the 'fever of ideas' there at the time, that the middle classes in Sinn Féin, led by Arthur Griffith, the *bête noire* of labour nationalists due to his opposition to Larkin and the workers in 1913, would 'duck out' of the independence struggle once some extension of Home Rule was offered and that the working class would then take over and push forward towards a workers' republic. He took the radical rhetoric of Irish labour leaders at this time at face value. 'It seemed to me', O'Donnell said later, 'that the working class was awaiting its hour.'[24] He saw his own role now as helping to build the union and the strength of labour so that it would be ready when the fateful moment came. He left Liberty Hall in October 1918, as an organizer with a roving commission covering Ulster (outside of Antrim and Down), and by February 1919 had been involved in forty-eight wage movements and three strikes. Two of those strikes were historic affairs – the occupation of Monaghan Asylum and the Caledon Mill strike.

The attendants and nurses at Monaghan Asylum had joined the Irish Asylum Workers' Union in early 1918. They had won a pay rise as a result of a week's strike in March, but many issues remained unresolved, not least a ninety-three hour working week. In December the asylum workers approached O'Donnell (the IAWU had no full-time officials) to negotiate on their behalf. He agreed, following ITGWU practice in helping out a weaker union while strengthening his own union's position in the town. He entered negotiations with the Asylum Committee, but they broke down on O'Donnell's demand for equal pay rises for women workers. On 23 January 1919 the staff went on strike but continued to provide emergency cover. Some workers wished to cut off food supplies to the asylum, but O'Donnell devised a better tactic: on 28 January the entire workforce occupied the building and ran the asylum with O'Donnell as 'governor'. Armed police laid siege as the workers raised the red flag and were the first of over one hundred groups of Irish workers in 1919–20 to adopt the term 'soviet'. The *Voice of Labour* hailed a new tactic. (As Greaves has pointed out, however, this was not a syndicalist 'take and hold' operation, but a means of taking industrial action without withdrawing labour. It was essentially a strike tactic, though with undeniable political overtones, and in all cases of 'soviets' up to 1921, the employers' property was returned once demands had been met.)[25] Negotiations were held, with the local priest acting as intermediary, and on 3 February the strike and occupation ended in victory for the workers. The working week was reduced to fifty-six hours, married attendants could now leave the premises after work, and a pay rise, equal for both men and women, was secured. The strike was a triumph also for O'Donnell and the ITGWU, which supplanted the Workers' Union (WU) as the main union in the town; the WU secretary and most of its Monaghan members joined the ITGWU, as did many other workers in the area, Catholic and Protestant. O'Donnell's deputy in the occupation had been the asylum carpenter, Willie Hare, a local Orangeman who helped to bring many more Protestant workers into the union. The Belfast engineering strike of January 1919 had shaken the British establishment in Ireland, and the senior British official in Ireland, Lord French, regarded the emergence of a united labour movement as a greater threat than Sinn Féin. Hare encouraged O'Donnell to establish a branch in the staunchly Orange town of Caledon, County Tyrone. This led to the historic Caledon Mill strike of February–April 1919, which ended in defeat and setback for the ITGWU.[26]

O'Donnell recruited workers in the local Fulton Mill in Caledon and on 21 February 220 workers went on strike following the sacking of two union members. He sought to transcend sectarianism in the face of the mill owner's efforts to beat the Orange drum, establishing a band with Orange and Catholic bandsmen and a 'citizen police force' to defend the pickets. He was happy to parade behind Union Jacks until they gave way to red flags. There was a nightly 'Red Flag procession' in the town, with 'No Surrender' emblazoned on one side of the flag and 'Up the Irish Transport' on the other. This 'flag that can thus unite our Irish workers', wrote O'Donnell, 'is the flag we want'. There were frequent clashes with the police and scabs, and Peadar was twice the victim of beatings. Orangemen on strike were victimized and the Unionist establishment portrayed the strike as a Sinn Féin attempt to 'cause strife in the Unionist ranks through the Labour class'. Sectarianism (and poverty) won out and the strike ended in defeat after ten weeks; however, a group of over forty Protestant workers refused to leave the union to return to work, and left for Yorkshire singing 'The Red Flag'. (Five years later, when he was imprisoned in the Curragh, O'Donnell was touched to receive greetings from members of that group who had maintained their association in England.)[27]

O'Donnell had made Monaghan town his base from the time of the asylum strike. He lodged with Charlie Emerson, the local IRA leader (the Volunteers were becoming known as the IRA during 1919) and joined up in August 1919. There was a close association between the Volunteers and the Transport Union across the country, with a pattern of joint membership and co-operation. O'Donnell had remained in contact with his group in Liberty Hall, and heard that one by one Archie Heron and the others were joining up. In the absence of a Citizen Army with a coherent strategy in the newly militarized circumstances, he assumed that this was the 'policy': to join the IRA and exert sufficient influence within it so that it would be in a position to push past the 'Home Rule settlement' for which the middle-class nationalist leadership would inevitably settle.[28] The Monaghan IRA engaged in little activity before February 1920, when they captured the RIC barracks at Ballytrain, the first barracks in Ulster and the third in the country to be taken. O'Donnell took part, as one of thirty members of the Monaghan brigade led by brigade commander Eoin O'Duffy.[29]

He had continued to concentrate on his union activities, but was obviously frustrated at the lack of an appropriate organizational expression for his politics. This frustration revealed itself at this time in his doomed efforts to kick-start ICA units and SPI branches. In late 1919, following a successful near general local strike in Monaghan, he commented to a colleague that they were making fools of themselves 'putting out one set of capitalists to put in another'. He formed a Citizen Army unit, but disbanded it after a month after he had to intervene to stop his 'soldiers' drowning a local strike breaker in a canal. During the summer he had made unsuccessful efforts to start branches of the Socialist Party in

Monaghan and Derry. He campaigned for the Labour Party in the January 1920 municipal elections in Cavan and Monaghan, where it made a relatively strong showing. While based in Derry in 1920 he again made an attempt to establish an ICA unit, but it disintegrated once sectarian violence broke out in the spring and summer, with members returning to their sectarian camps.[30]

The strike in Monaghan occurred in October 1919 and involved labourers and carters coming out against six of the town's employers. The workers controlled the town for five days, winning a six-shilling increase all round. 'The proletariat', wrote O'Donnell, 'have fought shoulder to shoulder under their own flag. The capitalist game of "divide and conquer" met with a serious reverse when all the town workers abandoned their fancy colours and united under the Red.'[31] He continued to push a class perspective in an increasingly polarized political situation; he criticized Sinn Féin and Unionists alike, pointing out that neither Unionist nor nationalist employers paid their workers extra because of their political sympathies.[32] However, this was a losing battle as the ITGWU's 'resolute Ulster campaign found itself sided into the nationalist ghetto'.[33] Branch numbers peaked in 1920 and went into decline thereafter. The strength of the position of the British-based unions in the North and the limited opportunities for expansion were highlighted by the experience of Derry, where O'Donnell was based from late 1919.[34]

He had established an ITGWU branch among cinema workers in Derry in January 1919, but subsequent progress was slow. An opportunity to win over the city's dockworkers, members of the National Union of Dock Labourers, was lost when Liberty Hall refused the workers' demand (supported by O'Donnell) that their secretary be given a union position. Labour leaders in Derry were conservative and associated with the old Irish Party and the British-based unions that had long dominated the city. They refused the ITGWU affiliation to the Derry Trades Council. Relations between the ITGWU and British-based unions became strained as it became involved in poaching members – the only route of expansion but ultimately counterproductive – and was sucked into the developing sectarian tension. O'Donnell admitted years later that his union's entry into Derry was mistaken 'and ultimately divisive. Unionization in Derry was already adequate and the ITGWU's identification with Irish nationalism', coinciding with the outbreak of hostilities between the IRA and British authorities, 'only served to heighten divisions between workers of different political and religious persuasions'.[35] He became involved in a particularly bitter dispute in summer of 1920 when 7,000 shirt cutters were laid off. Many were not unionized while those that were did not receive full strike pay from their union (the Amalgamated Society of Tailors and Tailoresses), while the trades council did nothing. O'Donnell negotiated a settlement, raised funds and publicly attacked the Derry trade union movement for its lack of support for the women workers. He also declared it his intention to 'smash every Cross-Channel union in Derry'.[36] The situation deteriorated as the Ulster Unionist Labour Association placed advertisements in newspapers calling on Protestants not to join the ITGWU. That group was responsible for the expulsion (on sectarian and political grounds) of 7,410 workers from their jobs in 1920. According to O'Donnell, its activities were fatal to the progress of the Transport Union in the North. The ITGWU supported the Sinn Féin-led boycott of Belfast goods, there was a retaliatory boycott by Protestants, and O'Donnell's words of the previous October regarding class unity seemed increasingly at odds with the situation as it was actually developing.[37] The battle lines that were being drawn in Ireland at this juncture were not those of the class war, and O'Donnell was moving inexorably towards full involvement in the military struggle against British rule.

Sectarian conflict in Derry climaxed in the riots of June 1920 when twenty people died in a week; the first fatality of the war of independence in Derry came in May when the IRA killed an RIC man. Curfews were imposed and British troops patrolled the streets. In the late summer of 1920 O'Donnell took command of the Second Battalion of the Donegal IRA, which covered northeast Donegal and Derry city. In November he received a tip-off from an RIC man (a member of the Irish Police and Prison Officers' Union, which O'Donnell had helped to establish) that he was about to be arrested and he went on the run. So ended his trade union activity; Peadar O'Donnell was henceforth a full-time IRA man.[38]

The 'stormy petrel of the Transport Workers', as a Derry newspaper dubbed him, had served the union well as a formidable organizer who made a major contribution to its short-lived growth in Ulster.[39] From a starting point of three branches in the province in June 1918, the union had ten by the end of the year and peaked at thirty-one in April 1920. This was the work of O'Donnell and just one other organizer, though his brother Frank was brought briefly on board between January and April 1919. However, the strength of the British-based unions, the union's increasing association with Catholic nationalism, and some poor decisions by the union leadership (such as the failure to recruit the Derry dockers) combined to limit and ultimately undo the success that had been achieved. Branch numbers fell to nineteen in 1921, fourteen in 1923 and by 1925 it was back to its original three branches.[40] The rapid expansion of the union meant that organizers like O'Donnell worked almost autonomously, developing tactics (such as the asylum occupation) on their own initiative. He occasionally acted without union authorization, as in the Monaghan strike of October 1919, which he led to victory despite repudiation from Liberty Hall. As McCabe points out, the intensity of his organizing activity gave him little time to work out a political programme or an alternative general strategy to the leadership. He did not speak at either the 1919 or 1920 Irish Trade Union Congresses, which he attended as a delegate for the Cavan Trades Council.[41] In the absence of a revolutionary party or organization that could or would attempt to explicitly link the labour and national struggles, and expose the limitations of the labour leadership in this regard, he went with the flow, hoping, indeed believing, that the labour leaders would come out eventually to take the lead in the developing struggle for independence. He was willing to wait and, as the situation militarized, he took the short step from the ITGWU into the IRA.

IRA active service

The opposition to British rule in Ireland in 1919–21 was actualized in three main ways: through the building of popularly accepted alternative state structures by Sinn Féin; through the actions of the organized working class; and through the armed activities of the IRA. O'Donnell's path was now the one of armed struggle. The attack on a police convoy by a Volunteer party at Soloheadbeg, County Tipperary on 21 January 1919, the day that the first Dáil assembled in Dublin, is generally taken as the starting point of the War of Independence. However, the pattern of widespread guerrilla warfare and increasing state repression did not establish itself until 1920. The conflict was entering an intense phase in late 1920 as O'Donnell was moving from being a part-time IRA volunteer to full-time active service. Terence MacSwiney, Lord Mayor of Cork, died on hunger strike on 25 October; Kevin Barry was hanged in Mountjoy jail on 1 November; ten British officers were killed in Dublin on 'Bloody Sunday', 21 November, leading to the killing of twelve civilians by British forces at a football match in Croke Park; a week later Tom Barry led his 'flying column' in the legendary Kilmichael ambush.

The flying columns (mobile units based in rural areas) were now emerging as a key element in IRA strategy.

In the third week of December 1920 Peadar O'Donnell attended an IRA meeting in the Shamrock Hall in Derry's Bogside. He announced his intention to set up a flying column and appealed for volunteers. Nine from the meeting joined him and they set off for Donegal on 29 December. When they reached the Rosses they were joined by Peadar's two brothers, Frank and Joe, and Con Boyle. They established their headquarters in Croveigh, a mountainy townland east of Dungloe.[42] The column joined up with Joe Sweeney's IRA unit to derail a troop train at Meenbanad in January 1921 and shot up another one at Crolly. They rarely engaged the enemy directly and kept on the move, setting up roadblocks, cutting telegraph wires and blocking rail tracks. In March there was an increase in incidents in Donegal. O'Donnell's column attacked the RIC barracks at Falcarragh, killing a policeman, while other sections of the Donegal IRA claimed two more RIC lives. British troops wrecked Donegal town, burned a creamery at Inver and killed a civilian in Malinbeg. In that month also the IRA grouped the four Donegal brigades into the First Ulster Division, under Frank Carney. O'Donnell was appointed O/C of the Second Brigade, covering east Donegal, the Inishowen peninsula and Derry city. He was unhappy with the lack of activity by the Derry battalion in the heavily militarized city and planned a series of simultaneous attacks on the British forces there on 1 April 1921. He travelled to Derry to co-ordinate the assault, which consisted of the bombing of an RIC station and an electricity plant, the shooting of a policeman, and a sniper attack on a British army post. An RIC man, two soldiers and two civilians were wounded. With the police hunting for him, O'Donnell slipped out of the city and returned to Donegal.[43] He left behind not only three fatalities, but a resentful Derry IRA leadership, which had not been consulted by O'Donnell and had their policy of keeping Derry quiet rudely disrupted as the police and army wreaked revenge. In general, O'Donnell's approach was that casualties were not important; what mattered was 'to make government impossible'.[44]

On 5 April 1921 a thousand troops arrived in the Rosses as part of the British army's countrywide spring offensive against the IRA. Five days later O'Donnell narrowly avoided capture in a dawn raid on a safe house. With the authorities putting pressure on the IRA, relations between Peadar and other IRA leaders became strained. Although his column was supposed to be operating in north-east Donegal, it spent most of its time in the Rosses, in Joe Sweeney's territory, and the latter resented having to provide for O'Donnell's men. On 7 May the Divisional Commander, Frank Carney, whom O'Donnell held in low regard (the feeling was mutual), ordered his column not to engage the enemy and summoned Peadar to Derry. He delayed en route and he and two of his men were surprised by troops. He narrowly escaped, but had his arm broken by a bullet as he fled. His injury was tended to as he was moved from house to house throughout Donegal while British troops swarmed through the Rosses. One of his refuges was a glen house near Errigal mountain where a young islandwoman lived with her husband and mother-in-law. The dynamic between the women, and the large windows in the house later inspired his finest novel, *The Big Windows* (1955).[45]

On 16 May Carney was captured and imprisoned in Derry. He was replaced as O/C of the First Northern Division by Joe Sweeney, who blamed O'Donnell for an attack on an RIC patrol, which resulted in the death of one policeman and broke the local ceasefire that had been established. He was becoming increasingly annoyed by Peadar's refusal to take orders, including one to burn down Glenveagh Castle. He suspended O'Donnell and GHQ sent Liam Archer to investigate the dispute and the poor relations that had developed between O'Donnell and other senior officers. Officers of the Derry battalion were annoyed about not being informed in advance about the 1 April attacks, while Sweeney told Archer that O'Donnell was 'well-meaning but impractical'. Despite a negative report from Archer, Michael Collins retained O'Donnell as head of the brigade, though he did separate Derry from the brigade area.[46]

O'Donnell retained his radical outlook, and it led him to resist at least one aspect of Dáil/IRA activity in these years: it was not only British 'government' that he sought to make 'impossible' in his area, but the type of Irish 'government' that moved in to replace it. Sinn Féin extended its power gradually as the British administrative, justice and policing systems became non-operational in large parts of the country. Labour arbitration courts were established in June 1919, and in 1920, courts of justice and land courts: the dual aim was to displace British administration and to quell and contain class unrest. The conservative dynamic of Sinn Féin, and its wish to suppress class antagonism in the name of 'the nation', was revealed as its courts were used against landless labourers and smallholders who had been involved in land seizures and cattle drives. In the majority of cases the courts came down in favour of landlords and property owners, and in general supported the socio-economic status quo, while the IRA was used as a police force to enforce the courts' decisions. O'Donnell saw in the land seizures the re-ignition of Fenian radicalism, but Sinn Féin used the IRA 'to patrol estate walls, enforce decrees for rent, arrest and even order out of the country leaders of local land agitations'.[47] He put a halt to the use of IRA men in his brigade for this purpose, which in turn stopped the Dáil courts from functioning in north-east Donegal.[48]

By the summer of 1921, the IRA was suffering setbacks and losses in Donegal, and O'Donnell was forced to disband his column because of the imprisonment of five of its members. Arrests, deaths and ammunition shortages were all taking their toll, in Donegal as much as in the rest of the country. The British were also suffering casualties and the tide of British and American opinion was turning against an increasingly dirty war in Ireland. The British government invited republican representatives to a peace conference in London, and on 11 July 1921 a truce was called.

2

'I'm in the wrong war!'
1921–1925

During the six months between the end of the war and the signing of the Anglo-Irish Treaty, the IRA maintained its structure and continued to organize and train. The uneasy peace also saw an upsurge in strikes and occupations by workers, taking advantage of a situation where employers were vulnerable in the absence of a strong state apparatus to back them. O'Donnell could move about openly for the first time in eight months and he spoke at a number of ITGWU-organized gatherings. He saw his task, within the IRA and generally, as being to 'build up the consciousness of the people; to get ready for the next political push of which we were a mere manifestation. I looked upon the army as a train that must be kept upon the right track and not let go down a siding.'[1] The IRA leadership in Dublin was meanwhile organizing training camps around the country and a young officer called Todd Andrews (later a leading member of Fianna Fáil) was sent to Donegal in late September 1921 to take charge of training in Dungloe.

At their first gathering nineteen-year-old Andrews nervously read his lecture and then invited one of the commanders, who seemed rather older than the rest, to comment. Peadar O'Donnell, then twenty-eight years old, stood up and poured out 'a stream of words arranged in fluent, well balanced sentences full of striking imagery and laced with quotations from James Connolly'. Andrews was struck dumb, and O'Donnell took over the direction of the meeting and subsequently helped the youngster to finish the two-week course. When it finished, O'Donnell took him to meet his mother: 'It was easy to see', recalled Andrews, 'where Peadar got his intelligence and warmth.' He was then given a tour of the Rosses during which O'Donnell introduced him to the idea of socialism in an Irish context, the first time that he had been exposed to the social revolutionary potential of the struggle in which he was involved: 'While it lasted and while Peadar's spell was on me, I was fascinated by these new ideas. Alas! When I said goodbye to Peadar at Letterkenny the vision he had evoked for me vanished. I reverted to the 'Aisling' which Pearse had created for the nation.'[2]

As Andrews was being given his tour of the Rosses in October 1921, Michael Collins, Arthur Griffith and the rest of the Irish delegation were leaving for London to begin the two-month-long negotiations that would result in the Anglo-Irish Treaty. O'Donnell fully expected the outcome to be a 'sell-out' by the middle-class leadership of the independence movement; he assumed, however, that this would be the moment in the struggle when the labour leadership would seize the initiative. He told a public meeting in Derry in November: 'The middle classes are the nervous peace seekers, who fear the advance of proletarian power more than they abhor the old tyranny'.[3]

The Treaty

The Treaty was signed on 6 December 1921. Under its terms, an Irish Free State with dominion status was to be established, with members of its parliament taking an oath to the British king. The Free State had to service the British public debt and the British retained control of the ports of Berehaven, Cobh and Lough Swilly. It also provided for a boundary commission to decide on the future of the border, but in the interim Northern Ireland remained intact. Sinn Féin and the Dáil were divided on the question of whether to approve the Treaty. The republican opposition was led by Eamon de Valera, President of the Republic, and focused on the oath of allegiance. The alternative offered by de Valera was 'Document No. 2', based on the idea of 'external association' with Britain rather than dominion status. On 7 January 1922 the Dáil voted to accept the Treaty by sixty-four votes to fifty-seven. De Valera resigned and was replaced as president by Griffith, while Collins headed up the Provisional Government responsible for implementing the Treaty. The split in Sinn Féin, and in the popular front that it had become, was soon followed by a split in the IRA, leading to a bitter civil war. While nine out of the thirteen members of GHQ staff supported the Treaty, a majority of field commanders like O'Donnell, and of the rank and file, rejected it outright: it has been estimated that seventy to eighty per cent of the IRA in all was anti-Treaty.[4] O'Donnell's opposition incorporated the standard republican emotional revulsion and sense of betrayal into a broader class-based, anti-imperialist analysis. 'Here was a situation', he wrote some years later,

> where the British ruling class was ordering Republican Ireland to drop its claim to be an independent Republic, was ordering us to surrender to the Empire, to bow to Lloyd George's declaration that in the interest of the Empire Northern and Southern Ireland must not be permitted to unite, to agree to provide for the cost of the Black and Tan war, to tie ourselves to Britain's war plans through surrendering ports and accepting the overlordship of the British General Staff, to have our elected representatives swear loyalty to the ruling British monarch.[5]

He had expected no less from Griffith, who he saw as getting the deal the Irish propertied class desired, while Collins, in his eyes, 'had emerged from the Tan struggle with the outlook of a "Fenian Home Ruler" and the code of a tinker swapping donkeys at a fair; he was suspicious of what he was getting but contented himself that what he was giving was not an honest beast'.[6] The required response from the republican leadership, the response that would have maintained army unity and galvanized popular opposition, O'Donnell believed, was an outright rejection and unambiguous declaration of independence: face the treaty with 'the Republic'. Instead, de Valera 'attempted to improve the terms of the bargain between the Irish middle-class and British Imperialism, and the bewildered masses were thrown into confusion. Without document No. 2 the Treaty would have smashed against a solid Irish Republican Army.'[7]

O'Donnell went to Liberty Hall, expecting hostility to the settlement, but discovered to his horror that Labour's official position was one of neutrality, and that it was de facto backing the Treaty, betraying its leadership's 'predilection for consensus'.[8] The first organization to publicly reject the Treaty was the newly constituted Communist Party of Ireland (CPI). This had been formed in October 1921 following the successful take-over of the executive of the Socialist Party of Ireland (SPI) in the previous month by Bolshevists led by James Connolly's son, Roddy. It began publishing *Workers' Republic*, affiliated to the Communist International (Comintern) and changed the party name from Socialist to Communist in line with Comintern policy. Although there was a new wave of strikes and industrial militancy between the truce and the Treaty, Ireland's first Communist Party did not involve itself. In its search for the source of revolution in Ireland it positioned itself not amongst the militant working class, but between the Soviet Union and republicans in a fateful triangle that would become the dominant shape on the Irish left for years to come. The party immediately allied itself to de Valera, ignoring the limitations of his opposition and the nature of his politics. The communists believed that the fight for socialism could only begin once the (bourgeois) struggle for independence had been completed. O'Donnell had been a member of the SPI, but it is unclear whether he continued his membership into the new CPI. He denied any connection with it in later years, but he did write for the paper on a number of occasions and was twice claimed as a member in the *Workers' Republic*, claims he did not see fit to deny at the time.[9] The CPI was small and peripheral, but its thinking was influential on the emergent republican left, which came to prominence in the late 1920s with Peadar O'Donnell at its core.

The Treaty issue divided the nationalist movement and Irish society generally. Within Sinn Féin and the IRA, multiple factors and variables were at play in determining support or rejection (regional, personal, gendered, etc.),[10] but at the broader social level an undeniable class dimension was evident, which strengthened the class interpretation of socialists like O'Donnell but also highlighted their inability to mobilize opposition on that basis. Strong farmers, employers and the prosperous middle classes were strongly pro-Treaty, supported by the press and the Catholic hierarchy. Opposition came from small farmers, sections of the petty bourgeoisie, the rural proletariat and a proportion of the urban working class; the majority of the latter remained 'neutral' on the issue. The Treaty had nothing to offer workers as a class, consolidating, as it did, partition (which crucially weakened the Irish labour movement) and the existing social structures within both states. Syndicalist actions continued until 1923, but workers were not offered leadership or analysis from a socialist perspective. The labour leadership, as we have seen, went the conservative nationalist route, while left-republicans and the CPI were following the politically bankrupt and militarily inept IRA into the cul-de-sac of the Four Courts and civil war.

Towards civil war

In Donegal in early 1922, O'Donnell was involved in maintaining the structure and morale of his IRA units. The Provisional Government was establishing a professional army and police force from the ranks of the pro-Treaty IRA and both sides competed for the barracks and supplies left by the departing British forces. In March the government banned the planned upcoming IRA convention and Richard Mulcahy, the Minister for Defence, announced that any IRA officer attending would be dismissed. Over fifty senior officers, including O'Donnell, signed a public summons to volunteers to attend as planned. The convention, representing seventy to eighty per cent of the IRA, met on 26 March. Control of the new force was transferred from the Dáil to a new executive, and a temporary executive was elected to draft a new IRA constitution. The delegates reconvened on 9 April and elected an executive of sixteen, including Peadar O'Donnell, who was appointed commander of the newly formed First Northern Division.[11] On 13 April the Four Courts in Dublin was occupied and established as IRA headquarters. O'Donnell was based in east Donegal but was a frequent visitor to Dublin to attend executive meetings that Ernie O'Malley described as 'a bad dream', involving endless discussion but no attempt to define a clear-cut policy.[12] In early June O'Donnell moved to the Four Courts, where the executive was based. His later descriptions of the calibre of the IRA leadership at this time are unambiguous: 'rather pathetic'; 'bankrupt of ideas'; 'uninspired, confused and feckless'. He believed that the IRA leaders like Liam Lynch and Rory O'Connor were 'unsuitable for the decisions now thrust upon them'.[13] The executive had no alternative programme to offer beyond opposition to the Treaty, and failed to co-ordinate with the political opposition under de Valera. In O'Donnell's view, neither the militarists nor the politicians could perceive or 'reveal what play of social forces constituted the Treaty in terms that made sense to the republican mass'; they 'were the stuff that martyrs are made of, but not revolutionaries'.[14]

Efforts at finding a compromise that would avert the danger of civil war continued between April and June, when an election was due. A truce between the two armies was announced on 4 May and, on the political front, an election pact was agreed between de Valera and Collins on 20 May, whereby elected candidates from both wings of Sinn Féin would form a coalition and the election would not be a referendum on the Treaty. Negotiations aimed at securing army unity resulted in an agreement which was rejected by a majority of the IRA executive, including O'Donnell, who believed that the Free Staters were playing for time, weakening the resolve of republicans and fomenting division amongst them while strengthening their own position and building their army. The results of the 'Pact election', in which the pro-Treaty panel won a majority, were claimed by the government as an endorsement of the Treaty, though republicans rejected this interpretation. On 22 June

Sir Henry Wilson, a Unionist MP, was assassinated in London. The British government wrongly blamed the Four Courts IRA and, threatening an assault by British troops, demanded action by the Provisional Government. With the executive still divided on the way forward, it was decided on 25 June that a fight against the common enemy in the North (where it was believed Catholics would be subject to further punitive measures following the Wilson killing) was the surest way to reunite republicans. O'Donnell was to lead a section to the North, and on 26 June a party left the Four Courts to seize cars to transport the convoy. One of the party, senior IRA man Leo Henderson, was arrested, and in response the IRA kidnapped J. J. O'Connell, deputy chief of staff of the pro-Treaty army. The Provisional Government now had the pretext to act and, as O'Donnell and his party were preparing to set off, the decision was taken to attack the Four Courts. Eighteen-pounder guns supplied by the British were positioned across the river and, on the morning of Wednesday 28 June 1922, the bombardment began.[15]

During the early stages of the bombardment, O'Donnell stood with Liam Mellows watching workers making their way along the quays. They discussed Connolly, and the role he would have envisaged for the labour movement in the situation 'the Republic' was now in. 'My God, Mellows,' O'Donnell remembers saying, 'I'm in the wrong war!'[16] Despite this moment of revelation, it was, it seems, too late to do anything about it. Confusion and delay prevented the arrival of IRA reinforcements from outside Dublin. Paddy O'Brien, the Four Courts O/C, wanted the executive to leave, but they refused, choosing instead to make their stand. On Friday morning the building caught fire and the garrison surrendered. The prisoners, numbering about 150 in all, were imprisoned in Mountjoy jail, where Peadar O'Donnell would spend the next twenty-one months of his life.

Mountjoy

In the early hours of 1 July 1922 O'Donnell was thrown into his cell. Initial feelings of panic and fear passed quickly and he settled into his new surroundings, gradually caught up in the 'whirling restlessness of jail life'.[17] The prisoners took control of their section of the prison, breaking down walls between cells and springing the cell doors to allow free association. The four wings of Mountjoy were soon filled with IRA prisoners; prisoner-of-war status was grudgingly conceded by the Provisional Government after weeks of protests, and a central administration was established in O'Donnell's C wing. The charismatic Liam Mellows was a dominant presence. He organized classes, concerts and games and was idolized by the young prisoners and by O'Donnell himself. They met often as members of the IRA executive in the jail and did many fatigue duties together. A group developed around Mellows, based in the cell he shared with Joe McKelvey, which held long discussions on future policies and tactics. Those involved included Peadar O'Donnell, Seamus Breslin (another former ITGWU official), Richard Barrett, Eamon Martin (who would later help O'Donnell on *The Bell*) and Walter Carpenter of the CPI.[18]

Carpenter had been among the CPI activists who had joined IRA and Citizen Army units in the armed exchanges and occupation of buildings in Dublin following the fall of the Four Courts. The brief foray into armed action was abandoned once the republican retreat from Dublin began and the party turned again to politics, and specifically to influencing the republican movement. The CPI argued that the republican campaign needed to be broadened, 'from a military to a military and social struggle'. By this it did not mean engagement with the workers' struggles, which were continuing apace, but the adoption of a political programme that would bring workers and small farmers to the republican side.[19] In early July 1922 Roddy Connolly, party president, had gone to London and collaborated with Michael Borodin of the Comintern in drafting a new radical (though not communist) social programme, which they hoped republican leaders would adopt. The programme proposed nationalization, land division, free housing and social services, as well as the arming of workers. Connolly returned to Ireland and on 26 July brought his proposals to Liam Lynch, IRA chief of staff, who was based in County Cork. He urged Lynch to establish a civilian government in Cork city and proclaim the CPI programme. Lynch bluntly told Connolly that he was a soldier, not a politician, and no action was taken.[20]

The course of the Civil War in these early days involved a pattern of barrack occupation by both sides as they consolidated their areas. The republicans held most of the west and the 'Munster Republic', south of a line from Limerick to Waterford. The conflict became entirely militarized as the Provisional Government devised an aggressive war plan and built up its army and armaments. Republican strategy was predominantly defensive, though the IRA vastly outnumbered the Provisional Government forces in the early stages of the Civil War and could have gained the upper hand had it taken the offensive from the outset. The defensive strategy adopted by the IRA was fatal and it was unable to maintain its hold on barracks and towns as the state army, with its superior firepower, quickly gained the upper hand.

The only senior republican to respond to the CPI proposals was Mellows. From the time of the truce, he had been of the opinion that republicans needed a social policy and had been tentatively formulating his own ideas. In Mountjoy in July–August 1922 his ideas were sharpened under the influence of Carpenter and, more importantly, O'Donnell, a CPI sympathizer at least, if not, as the party claimed, a member. Of possible significance also was the fact that the person in charge of smuggling in communications was Lile O'Donel, who had apparently joined the CPI in early 1922. (Peadar was in charge of outward communications, and they eventually married in 1924.) Copies of the *Workers' Republic* were read and discussed by Mellows and his circle. The issues of 22 and 29 July and 12 August contained details of the Connolly/Borodin programme, which Mellows incorporated into his own policy proposals. In August, Ernie O'Malley, who had escaped en route to Mountjoy and was becoming frustrated at the lack of clarification of the IRA's political, social and military aims, sent a request to Mellows for suggestions on political direction.[21] He smuggled out his ideas in a document that has become known as 'Notes from Mountjoy'. A copy was captured and published in the *Irish Independent* on 21 September under red scare headlines, at a time when the government was in the process of introducing draconian new legislation. O'Donnell's influence on Mellows's thinking is generally acknowledged, but he was keen to clarify his role: 'De Valera and people tried to say that it was I that [induced] Mellows to write those notes . . . I didn't add anything to the content of his mind. But I certainly did make him write them.'[22]

On 26 August 1922 the *Workers' Republic* published an article by O'Donnell entitled 'The Imperial Labour Party', wherein he sought to encourage workers to pull behind the republicans. He argued that the Labour Party had abandoned Connolly and 'gone Imperial', due mainly to Labour Party leader Thomas Johnson. It was the workers in the IRA, O'Donnell argued, that were playing the part outlined by Connolly: 'Revolutions are not made by Street Soviets nor by cheap talk of Dying Later for Something Big. There is a Revolutionary position now.' He concluded by calling on the labour movement to throw its weight behind the IRA (and on the Irish Citizen Army to deport Tom Johnson!). By this time the Civil War had entered a new phase, with the adoption of guerrilla tactics by the republicans following the progress of government troops into its southern stronghold. It was an effective move and a military stalemate set in. One of the first casualties of the new tactic was Michael Collins, killed in an ambush in County Cork on 22 August.

During September, Mellows began a prison magazine, cleverly titled *The Book of Cells*, in which O'Donnell made his debut as a writer. He wrote a short story satirizing Provisional Government minister Desmond Fitzgerald ('He wore a faded cockney accent that he had rinsed in Oxford on the way to Rathmines and he always displayed the laundry tag.'),[23] and he and Mellows began to compete at satirizing the pretensions of other Free Staters like Ernest Blythe and Eoin MacNeill. These jottings opened up his creative ducts and memories of the islands came flooding back to him. It was during this period that he wrote the opening scene of what would be his first novel, *Storm* (1925). On 8 October an attempted mass escape failed, ending in a shoot-out in which one prisoner was killed and another wounded.[24] Two days later the Irish Catholic bishops issued a joint pastoral condemning resistance to the Provisional Government and prison chaplains began refusing the sacraments to prisoners who refused to submit to the authority of the nascent Free State regime.[25] There was angry reaction in Mountjoy, particularly at the refusal of priests to allow the dead bodies of republicans into churches. Bishops and priests were condemned and abused in unambiguous terms by the inmates, a level of anger later controversially portrayed by O'Donnell in his novel *The Knife* (1930). He carried his own resentment to his grave, and it was influential on his decision not to have his body brought into a church, or have a priest present at his funeral, despite his life-long Catholicism.[26] The Dáil assembled in September and passed the Public Safety Bill, known to republicans as the 'Murder Bill', empowering the army to establish military courts, which began to function from 15 October. All acts of war, and even the possession of arms and ammunition, were now punishable by execution. The meeting of the Dáil provoked renewed discussion on the formation of an alternative republican government. The first IRA executive meeting since the beginning of the war was held in Tipperary on 16 and 17 October. O'Donnell and the other imprisoned members were replaced and a 'government' was formed with de Valera as president. Liam Mellows was appointed Minister for Defence, but his policy suggestions were not discussed and the new body was purely symbolic.[27]

On 17 November four young IRA men were executed, followed the next day by well-known republican Erskine Childers. The prisoners in

Mountjoy had been getting back into their stride following the failed escape attempt, and O'Donnell was doing more and more writing. All changed utterly, however, with the news of the executions. The mood darkened and the jail became filled with 'a brooding spirit of vengeance' as prisoners planned reprisals.[28] Similar feelings infected republicans on the outside. On 30 November a general order was issued to IRA units to kill listed categories of Provisional Government supporters. The reprisal orders were acted on only once. On 7 December, the day after the Irish Free State came officially into existence, the Dublin No. 1 Brigade killed Seán Hales TD and wounded Pádraic Ó Máille TD. The cabinet then authorized the (unlawful) execution of four prominent republicans held in Mountjoy.[29]

On the night of 7 December, Peadar O'Donnell was attending a debate in Mountjoy on 'Women in Industry – Equal Pay for Equal Work'. The mood among the prisoners was relaxed, with 'no impending sense of doom';[30] they had just received news that a tunnel was making good progress towards the jail. After the debate they made their way back to their cells. O'Donnell stopped to tell Liam Mellows a joke, which he turned to share with his cellmate, Joe McKelvey. O'Donnell went to bed and awoke the next morning to the news that Mellows, McKelvey, Rory O'Connor and Dick Barrett had been taken from their cells the night before and executed that morning. The killings were greeted with shock and horror both outside and inside Mountjoy, but they appear to have deterred the further killing of TDs, and had a devastating effect on republican morale. O'Donnell was shattered with grief and anger, feeling the loss of Mellows in particular: 'the richest mind our race had achieved for many a long day had been spilled', and now the months spent in prison 'seemed to stretch in a grey, dull waste to the edge of the years that had been so alive'.[31] In early 1923 O'Donnell was transferred to Tintown No. 1 in the Curragh where, as senior officer, he was made O/C of the camp's 600 inmates.

O'Donnell and the CPI

It was becoming increasingly clear that the republican campaign was doomed, and the CPI concluded that its policy of concentrating on the republican movement had been mistaken. Roddy Connolly, who many in the party blamed for the concentration on influencing republicans to the neglect of workers' struggles, attended the Fourth World Congress of the Comintern in Moscow at the end of 1922. Comintern policy was that communist parties should fight for the most radical solution possible to the bourgeois democratic revolution, while simultaneously organizing the working class to struggle for its specific class interests, thus exposing the contradictions of the bourgeois nationalist project. While the CPI could be said to have pursued the first of those tasks, it had failed in the second and was criticized privately for this at the Congress.

On his return from Moscow, Connolly published a series of articles in the *Workers' Republic* in which he argued that the Free State was an advance on the previous position and that it might be possible to move from it directly to the workers' state. He called for concentration on building the labour movement and suggested that republicans should call off their armed struggle, form a Workers' Republican Party, take the oath and enter the Dáil. He claimed that this line was sanctioned by the Comintern, which caused dissension at the CPI Congress on 20 January 1923, as George Pollock, who had accompanied Connolly to Moscow, contradicted his claim. As a result, Connolly lost his place on the executive and his editorship of the paper, amid accusations that he had been 'bought out' by the Free State and the Labour Party.[32]

O'Donnell entered the debate with a response to Connolly's suggestions in the 3 February 1923 issue of *Workers' Republic*. The presentation and tenor of the piece suggests acceptance by the communists of O'Donnell as a significant figure in the debate, and his own regard for their ideological/political relevance (they were numerically insignificant). Again, the vexed question of his membership of the party arises. His opening remarks ('I am anxious to be clearly understood, and I give pretty fully here vital objections that make it impossible for me to reconcile our points of view') could be read to suggest that this marked his break from association with the first CPI, which would help to explain his subsequent dismissal of the party. The focus of his attack on Connolly was his perception that the latter had accepted the legitimacy of the Free State. He argued that, as British rule in Ireland was founded on a crime, and the Free State was a British institution, Irish people were morally obliged to oppose it. He broadened the terms of reference of the republican struggle by linking it to the global struggle against imperialism. 'Any settled order in Ireland under the Free State means the strengthening of the British Empire . . . the most powerful enemy of the struggling peoples of today.' Thus, to accept the Free State was to betray 'subject peoples all the world over'. He proposed that the time was ripe for the issuing of a republican constitution with a strong social policy, concluding that if republicans 'had no policy except to oppose

Imperialism I would take part in that resistance, and urge its continuance with my last breath'.

Connolly replied to O'Donnell in the same issue. He denied accepting the legitimacy of the Free State and said his policy was about the means and methods of struggling against it. Republican methods spelt defeat, and the adoption of a social programme at the current stage of the struggle was too little, too late. He dismissed O'Donnell's final comments as a 'policy of despair for a Communist. It's only a petit bourgeois would believe that, and I know you don't believe it, and that you'll abandon your policy of despair and line up to the true Communist position.' O'Donnell, however, retained his commitment to the republican struggle while the CPI, divided and increasingly neo-syndicalist in focus, descended towards oblivion.

The Curragh and Finner camps

The first four months of 1923 saw the linked disintegration of the IRA's military effort and republican morale. There were thirty-four executions in January alone and the Free State began to hold prisoners as hostages in their local areas, with death sentences to be carried out in the event of a republican attack. Peadar O'Donnell was soon to fall victim to this tactic. In the meantime he oversaw the start of a major tunnel in Tintown in the Curragh, through which seventy-three men eventually escaped. On 14 March he was shocked and saddened by the execution in Donegal of Charlie Daly and three others that had been carrying on the losing fight in the northwest. His brother Frank was among the few republicans still at large in Donegal, while the Free State forces were under the command of his old adversary, Joe Sweeney. Following the executions, the local press carried notices from Sweeney stating that republican prisoners would be held accountable for any further IRA actions.[33] On 17 March O'Donnell was brought, via Mountjoy, to Finner camp in Donegal and put in solitary confinement, with no reading materials and daily searches by the military police, the threat of execution hanging over him.[34] Fortunately for him, and possibly influenced by his predicament, what remained of the Donegal IRA launched no more significant attacks. In the meantime, a number of 'counter-terror' measures were taken. Peadar smuggled out a list to Frank naming those who were to be shot if he was executed, including Joe Sweeney. Lile O'Donel paid a visit to Labour Party leader Tom Johnson telling him he would be shot dead if anything happened to Peadar.[35] The republican campaign had been reduced to a policy of sabotage and arson by this stage and there were repeated calls from within the movement for peace initiatives to be taken, moves resisted by Liam Lynch. The daily bulletin of news and reports that O'Donnell began receiving from new prisoners made it clear that the IRA was broken and that this phase of the struggle was effectively drawing to a close.

His time over the next weeks was spent considering the nature and form of the next republican mobilization. In this regard, he made a crucial decision about his personal role:

> I know that I know the insides of the minds of the mass of the folk in rural Ireland: my thoughts are distilled out of their lives. Therefore, it is not my task to say anything new but to put words on what is in confused ferment in their minds. How would I say it? Write? I could try and I did . . . If I could say their lives out loud to these remnants of the Irish of history until they would nod their heads and say 'this is us!' A powerful, vital folk they are but too blasted patient; muling along carrying manure on their backs, draining bogs, blasting stones, while out beyond is their inheritance.[36]

He wrote a scene that later featured in *Islanders* (1927), and began a journey as a writer that would last until the 1980s, driven by the purpose formulated in solitary confinement in those closing months of the Civil War. He bemoaned the loss of Mellows as a focal point for the new mobilization, but then decided that 'collective genius' was a preferable option: 'The big thing to emphasize is that the stubborn splendour of the big mass of the people must be involved in the tactics of the Revolution: this heresy of the cult of armed men that brought Collins to imperialism and us to defeat must be overcome.'[37]

Liam Lynch was killed on 10 April 1923 and at an IRA executive meeting ten days later Frank Aiken was appointed chief of staff. He announced a ceasefire and dump-arms order on 24 May. The Civil War was over, but the IRA had not surrendered and no peace deal had been negotiated. Prisoners and internees were not released and O'Donnell was among approximately 12,000 who remained behind bars. However, within a week of the ceasefire his life in Finner changed dramatically. The fear of execution was lifted and he suddenly had access to books, letters and writing materials. He remained there until early August, when he was transferred back to Mountjoy.

Election and hunger strike

The Free State government, seeking to consolidate its military victory and legitimize the new regime, called a general election for 27 August 1923. On 1 August a Public Safety Act maintained emergency powers and authorized the continued incarceration of prisoners and internees. Military defeat had pushed 'the politicians' to the forefront in the republican camp, and de Valera successfully argued for participation in the election on an abstentionist platform. The pro-Treatyites had formed a new party, Cumann na nGaedheal, while republicans ran on a Sinn Féin ticket. O'Donnell was nominated by Sinn Féin to stand in Donegal, and his candidature provoked some interesting responses. The CPI claimed that he was a member of the party and was standing as a 'Worker Republican' candidate. Donnchadh MacNiallghuis of the IRA declared that O'Donnell's candidature did not have the sanction of the IRA, provoking a response from chief of staff Frank Aiken, who clarified that the army had nothing to do with the election and 'he would have been sanctioned by the IRA had such been necessary'.[38] O'Donnell topped the republican poll and was elected. He later claimed that he was unaware of the CPI's sponsorship, and dismissed it as 'a gimmick to get on the bandwagon'.[39] Forty-three other republicans were also elected, while Cumann na nGaedheal won sixty-three seats. Sinn Féin had performed remarkably well given the circumstances and the results delighted O'Donnell and his fellow prisoners. They were suddenly awash with hope for the task of remobilization: 'the road back was going to be shorter than we dared hope'.[40]

In the autumn of 1923 the authorities in Mountjoy began withdrawing political status. There were escapes, attempted escapes and riots as prisoners expressed frustration with conditions and their continued incarceration. Matters reached a head on 13 October when the prisoners in Mountjoy began an ill-considered and hopeless mass hunger strike in support of their demand for unconditional release. O'Donnell was among those who argued for a strike, believing it would give 'the resistance outside', illustrated by the election result, 'something to rally around'.[41] The strike spread to the other prisons until, by 23 October, an estimated 8,000 prisoners were refusing food. The protest was unplanned and uncoordinated and, with such huge numbers involved, inevitably began to crumble within weeks. O'Donnell was among the several hundred that held out, remaining on strike for forty-one days. After the first week, the authorities began to break up the

Mountjoy contingent who had initiated the strike, and O'Donnell was among those transferred to Kilmainham.[42]

In his prison memoirs, he recalled that 'the greatest sensation of a hunger strike is the exhilaration the mind achieves; it becomes so lit up that you cannot but be aware of its blaze and brilliance'.[43] He revelled in the mental clarity that physical hunger provoked, and the ideas formed in Finner about his own role in releasing the hidden potential of the Irish dispossessed were copperfastened:

> I saw that it is not that people inject anything new, they detonate qualities that are sulking in a haze . . . There are forces awaiting release, qualities awaiting a touch, that we never sense, and we live not in the wide sense of our inherent capacities but in the narrow laneways of yesterday's dead inherited murmurings.[44]

As the number of hunger-strikers whittled down to the hundreds, O'Donnell realized that the whole project was having the opposite effect to what he had hoped: rather than rallying the resistance, it was now 'tearing the heart' out of it, sapping morale and causing division inside and outside the prisons. The authorities remained unyielding about the pledge to the Free State that each prisoner would have to sign before release, thus facilitating a rekindling of the sense of solidarity amongst republicans that had been disintegrating under the pressure of the strike.[45] In his fifth week without food, O'Donnell was confined to bed and began suffering from violent headaches and maddening itches. Two hunger-strikers died on 20 and 22 November and O'Donnell helped to organize a co-ordinated end to the strike the following day. He appointed himself nurse to Ernie O'Malley, badly affected due to recent injuries. 'Peadar is a great character', O'Malley wrote to Molly Childers on 28 November,

> and gaol has improved him enormously. He has been rebaptised in his republican faith, has grown less argumentative, less verbose, and more charitable in his socialistic outlook. He is rather brilliant, I think, and is evidently well read as regards philosophy, pychology (can't spell it), social problems, economics, etc. so I propose learning as much as I can from him.[46]

Escape and marriage

There was no mass release of prisoners following the hunger strike, but the government soon abandoned its pledge demand and began a process of release by 'dribble' in December 1923.[47] O'Donnell was transferred to Harepark camp in the Curragh where reorganization of the republican forces became the main theme of prison life. Many retained the spirit of vengeance born at the height of the executions, and it took much persuasion by O'Donnell and others to convince them that reorganization, and not assassination, was the way forward. The dribble of releases continued but, despite the inevitability of release, O'Donnell was becoming 'fidgety' and 'restless'. He wrote to Lile O'Donel telling her of his intention to break out, adding another intention: 'If we get on as well when we meet as we do now, we should get married.'[48] She agreed, giving him added incentive to escape. A neighbour from the Rosses was a camp guard and he supplied O'Donnell with a Free State officer's uniform. He approached the gates in the early hours of 16 March 1924 and they were 'flung open'. He made his way to Dublin, then to Liverpool, from there to Belfast and on to the comparative safety of Donegal. He remained on the run over the next three to four months, until the declaration of an amnesty and the general jail releases in the autumn of 1924.[49]

Following his escape, he finally met Lile O'Donel in person. As he had hoped, they got on as well as they had in their clandestine communications and were married on 25 June 1924 in the Catholic church on Berkley Road in Dublin. The witnesses included Peadar's brother Frank, soon to join thousands of other republicans in exile in America; Mary MacSwiney, one of the foremost republican women of her generation; Fiona Plunkett, leading Cumann na mBan activist and member of another famous republican family, and Sinéad Bean de Valera.[50] Their honeymoon in a country hotel near Dublin was cut short when O'Donnell, still a wanted man, was recognized by a fellow guest on their first morning. They returned immediately to Dublin, where he lay low until the amnesty was declared.[51] They settled in Marlborough Road in the affluent suburb of Donnybrook in Dublin. Significantly, Lile's inherited wealth meant that O'Donnell could now devote himself fully to political activity and his linked writing career, and live the life of that favourite bogey-man of police reports, the 'professional agitator'.

O'Donnell, republicanism and communism, 1924–5

O'Donnell was centrally involved in both the political and military wings of the republican movement as it flapped about in search of direction in the hostile environment of the consolidating Free State in 1924–5. The 'wreckage of the IRA' met in the summer of 1924 and began a process of reorganization and morale restoration. In an effort to develop civilian sympathy, all volunteers were urged to join Sinn Féin *cumainn* in order to rekindle the republican spirit.[52] Sinn Féin, reinvented as the political wing of republicanism since June 1923, had expanded rapidly in its first year. It refused to recognize the institutions of the Free State and set about unsuccessfully replicating the alternative state structures established by the previous manifestation of Sinn Féin in 1919–21. Republicans maintained their own executive, legislature, judicial system and army, and provided limited welfare and educational services.[53] Despite these efforts, as O'Donnell pointed out at the time, republican government remained little more than 'a rumour'; he argued that republicans should become 'a creative force in a new industrial effort', giving concrete shape to the alternative government, and made a series of practical suggestions as to how this might be done.[54] Sinn Féin had published an embryonic economic programme in March 1924 which, unlike O'Donnell's proposals, was strong on aspiration and generalities and weak on practicalities and specifics. More significantly, from O'Donnell's left-wing perspective, it reiterated the traditional Sinn Féin commitment to 'the well-being and prosperity of all classes of the Irish community'.[55]

From September 1923 until July 1924 republican deputies who were not in prison or on the run gathered monthly to discuss and develop policy, in conjunction with Sinn Féin. O'Donnell began attending following his escape from prison. By July the majority of the republican leadership, including de Valera, had been released and on 7–8 August 1924 the surviving members of the Second Dáil (of August 1921), together with republicans who had been elected in the elections of June 1922 and August 1923, assembled in Sinn Féin headquarters for the first full gathering of Comhairle na dTeachtaí, the Council of Deputies. The republican position was that the Free State government was a usurping authority that had taken power in a *coup d'état*; the *de jure* legislature and government was represented by the Second Dáil (of August 1921). De Valera proposed that Comhairle na dTeachtaí 'act as the Council of State and be the actual government of the Country', while the Second Dáil, for formal acts and the sake of continuity, would continue as the *de jure* government.[56]

O'Donnell soon came to the conclusion that 'nothing good could come of this body, for here was the same climate of ideas as in 1918; the same impatience with every gesture towards agitation on social issues.'[57] At the August meeting he argued fruitlessly that a way should be found to bring workers into the movement.[58] Five by-elections were held in November 1924, resulting in a significant increase in the republican vote since August 1923 and the capture of two seats for Sinn Féin. It won a further two seats in the nine by-elections held in March 1925, bringing to forty-eight the number of republicans absenting themselves from the de facto locus of political power in Leinster House, where the Labour Party and Farmers' Party represented the opposition to the Cumann na nGaedheal government. Despite its modest electoral successes, Sinn Féin went into decline from late 1924 as it suffered a linked decrease in both income and membership. Emigration, unemployment and discrimination were reducing the numbers of activists and hampering political and military reorganization. The drop in support in the 1925 by-elections strengthened de Valera's belief that abstentionism would have to be abandoned, and throughout the summer and autumn of 1925 rumours about a 'new departure' persisted.[59] However, it was not only Sinn Féin's failure to maintain its constituency that appears to have motivated de Valera, but the fear that a form of class politics, whereby 'the national interest as a whole will be submerged in the clashing of rival economic groups',[60] would become institutionalized, with the Labour Party representing the growing opposition to the increasingly reactionary and conservative Cumann na nGaedheal government.[61]

The possibility of developing a revolutionary socialist opposition was hampered by (besides the larger structural and cultural factors) the egotism of Jim Larkin, the influential Comintern's shifting priorities and the continuing adherence of socialists like O'Donnell to the IRA model. The CPI had continued to disintegrate, and when Larkin returned from the US in 1923 he established the Irish Worker League (IWL), which the Comintern recognized as its official section in Ireland. It dissolved the CPI and instructed its members to join the IWL, a loosely structured organization rather than a Leninist party. In June 1924 Larkin attended the Fifth World Congress of the Comintern and was elected to its executive committee (ECCI). In his absence his supporters had broken from the ITGWU and formed the Workers' Union of Ireland (WUI), which soon affiliated to the Profintern (the Comintern's trade union counterpart). Lenin had died in January 1924 and the international communist movement was now coming under the influence of Stalin and his developing policy of 'socialism in one country', which prioritized the interests of the Soviet Union rather than the cause of world revolution.[62]

The prospects for building a mass communist movement in Ireland in the mid-1920s, with Larkin at its core, were not as poor as they may appear in retrospect. While the labour movement was in retreat and decline, there was much rank and file disillusionment with the failure of the reformist leadership to resist the anti-worker policies of the Free State government. The IWL attracted 500 workers to its founding rally; 16,000 workers defected from the ITGWU to the WUI, while 5,000 were affiliated to what has been called 'a third locus of communism', the Dublin Trades Council.[63] The anti-communism that characterized the early 1930s had not yet developed, while Sinn Féin, with its continued abstentionist inertia and disregard for socio-economic policies, was failing to harness opposition to the Free State regime. The left in the IRA, in the meantime, was gaining in influence, seeking direction and willing to develop mutually advantageous relations with the communist movement. Ireland in the mid-1920s was ripe for a political alternative to Cumann na nGaedheal, but, as we shall see, it was not the left that would ultimately provide it.

Bob Stewart, the Communist Party of Great Britain (CPGB) representative on the ECCI, arrived in Ireland to help Larkin build the party. The groundwork included the establishment of two Comintern front organizations, aimed at drawing republicans towards communism, and workers away from the official labour leadership. A branch of the International Class War Prisoners' Association was established to support republican prisoners, but most of its work was in support of prisoners in Northern Irish and British jails. Although it collapsed in 1927, it was revived again in 1929 as the Irish Labour Defence League. The other group was Workers' International Relief (WIR), which focused on food relief for smallholders in the west enduring near-famine conditions. O'Donnell and other prominent republican figures like Hanna Sheehy Skeffington joined the executive along with Stewart, Larkin and other IWL leaders. While some practical relief was distributed, the WIR failed to gain a political foothold for the communists. The efforts to found a communist party were scuppered when Larkin, who was at loggerheads with the CPGB and appears to have been using international communist support for his own ends, withdrew his support at the last minute in May and again in October 1925.[64]

With neither Sinn Féin/Comhairle na dTeachtaí nor the communists offering socially radical opposition to the Free State regime (the former for political reasons, the latter because of organizational difficulties), O'Donnell threw his energies into the IRA. He came to the conclusion that it needed to break from the purists in Sinn Féin so that it could 'make its way into vital association with the people'. This could only be achieved, he concluded, by the IRA 'giving itself a role in struggles on concrete issues, which alone could expose the interests with which the Treaty corresponded and create the forces for their overthrow'.[65] The IRA was still in a process of reorganization and in February 1925 de Valera and his ally, IRA chief of staff, Frank Aiken, had signed an agreement reasserting the role of the 'government' as the controlling authority for the army. However, O'Donnell was not alone in finding this state of affairs increasingly unsatisfactory. There was widespread disillusionment with the apparent futility of the political movement, highlighted by Sinn Féin's disastrous showing in the June 1925 local elections.[66] In the run-up to the IRA's first post-Civil War general army convention, O'Donnell suggested at an army council meeting that the IRA should declare itself independent, but received no support.[67] When he put forward a resolution to the same effect at the convention itself, however, it won overwhelming support.

The convention was held on 14–15 November 1925. A new streamlined constitution was adopted, which reasserted the primacy of armed force as the means to achieve the thirty-two county republic and gave the organization a more coherent structure.[68] Under the name of the Tirconnail battalion, O'Donnell put forward his resolution, which read:

> in view of the fact that the government has developed into a mere political party and has apparently lost sight of the fact that all energies should be devoted to the all-important work of making the army efficient so that the renegades who through a coup d'état assumed governmental powers in this country be dealt with at the earliest possible opportunity; the army of the Republic severs its connection with the Dáil and act under an independent executive, such executive to be given the power to declare war when, in its opinion, a suitable opportunity arises to rid the Republic of its enemies and maintain it in accordance with the proclamation of 1916.[69]

According to himself, 'an overwhelming decision against had almost been made'[70] when the rumours about the abandonment of abstentionism were raised. Aiken admitted that there had been informal talks along those lines amongst the leadership, provoking 'an outburst of pain and passion' directed against the Free State and anyone who would associate with it, and leading to a stampede vote in favour of the resolution.[71] Ironically, a proposal designed to distance the IRA from the purists was carried on the basis of revulsion against those who were considering abandonment of that same purism; ultimately, however, it was a vote against 'politics'. While the motion was clearly militaristic and generally anti-political in content, it was in intent specifically anti-parliamentary. Such subtle distinctions mattered little to the militaristic majority, for whom politics was politics – a time-wasting distraction from the real business of preparing for and engaging in armed struggle. When the vote for the new executive took place, Aiken and the other supporters of the 'new departure' were displaced. The new army council replaced Aiken with Andy Cooney as chief of staff. Peadar O'Donnell became a member of both the executive and army council of the 'new', autonomous IRA, an organization recommitted to the primacy of the nationalist armed struggle and as far away as ever from being a vehicle for (or the spearpoint of) class struggle that he wished it to become. 'There was endless argument on the Army Council', he recalled, 'between the claims of armed struggle and agitation', and, despite his best efforts, the former consistently triumphed.[72]

November 1925 was an eventful month for Peadar O'Donnell. Not only had he precipitated the split between Sinn Féin and the IRA (a move that made him understandably unpopular with many Sinn Féiners, and eased the road for de Valera's upcoming new departure), but his first novel, *Storm* (subtitled *A Story of the Irish War*) was published by the Talbot Press in Dublin. He had begun the book in Mountjoy in the autumn of 1922 and added to it during his continuing incarceration and after his escape. The disjointed process of its creation, as well as the fact that it was his first attempt at novel writing, contributed to its uneven and poor quality.

The storm of the title refers to the gales that struck the west coast of Ireland in November 1919, and metaphorically to the War of Independence. The strongly autobiographical central character, Eamon Gallagher, is a campaigning schoolteacher based on Arranmore who becomes a battalion commandant in the Anglo-Irish War. His story closely follows that of O'Donnell's in the war, except that Eamon dies heroically, and rather melodramatically, in the end. As a novel, this was easily his worst and it is of interest mainly for the insights it gives into O'Donnell's own feelings during the 'troubles', particularly the moral duty he felt to join the armed struggle. The author came to share the low opinion that most critics had of the book; he inserted a clause into his will forbidding a re-issue, and rarely, if ever, referred to *Storm* in the many talks he gave on his writing in later years. Despite its flaws, it sold a respectable 1,500 copies and marked the beginning of O'Donnell's literary career. He was now a 'writer', which gave him both added status in, and usefulness to, the republican movement, a higher public profile, and the confidence to develop his writing with the reflective and political purpose he had formulated in solitary confinement in Finner and on hunger strike in Kilmainham in 1923.

3

'My pen is a weapon'
1926–1931

The Sinn Féin *árd fheis*, which began three days after the IRA convention in November 1925, postponed a decision on the abandonment of abstentionism. However, within two months a special conference was called to finally decide the issue. The crucial factor in forcing the pace in the short term (the upcoming general election in 1927 provided the medium term impetus) was the signing of the Boundary Agreement on 3 December 1925 by the British, Northern Irish and Free State governments. Partition was now confirmed and copperfastened, and republicans had been helpless to oppose it. The special *árd fheis* opened on 9 March 1926. De Valera put forward a motion declaring abstentionism (in the absence of the oath) a matter of policy not principle. An amendment from vice-president Fr Michael O'Flanagan countered with the purist abstentionist position. The latter was narrowly carried by 223 to 218 votes; de Valera resigned as president of the party and two weeks later as president of the republican Dáil.[1] In April 1926 he and his followers established a new party, Fianna Fáil, which was formally launched in May.

O'Donnell attended the *árd fheis* in his capacity as a TD, and while he did not speak in favour of de Valera's proposal, he spoke against the amendment. The distinction was subtle but clear. While not wishing to follow de Valera's path, he opposed the elevation of abstentionism to the level of principle and welcomed the foundation of Fianna Fáil as 'a breath of fresh air into a world of make-believe'.[2] The split created space for radicals like himself to assume greater prominence in the IRA, not least in the area of publicity and propaganda. Following the 1923 election, Sinn Féin began publishing a weekly paper called *Sinn Féin*. On 18 June 1925 it was replaced by *An Phoblacht*, 'a weekly organ of Republican opinion', edited by the *Sinn Féin* editor, P. J. Little. In April 1926, following the Sinn Féin split, the IRA army council took over control of the paper and installed their 'writer in residence', Peadar O'Donnell, as editor to replace Little, who had gone with de Valera to become a founding member of Fianna Fáil.

He had no experience of editing and when he brought his first issue to the printers, he had the makings of two and a quarter papers. He soon learnt the ropes and, as he said, used the paper 'shamelessly, as though it was a private organ'.[3] Under the editorship of Little, *An Phoblacht* had differed little from its predecessor, *Sinn Féin*, and was characterized by pan-class nationalism, devotional Catholicism and Irish-Irelandism. Under O'Donnell, and his successor Frank Ryan, it developed a marked left-wing slant and became the most significant radical paper in post-independence Ireland. The cross-class approach was replaced by a socialist outlook, with an emphasis on class struggle in Ireland and internationally, while the religious articles became far less frequent. The main element of continuity was in the area of culture, where a protectionist, nativist, Irish-Ireland focus was maintained.[4] While O'Donnell used the paper to promote the many causes close to his heart, the main agitational use he made of it was to publicize and promote a struggle he initiated soon after he took over *An Phoblacht*: the campaign against the payment of land annuities.

O'Donnell, the land annuities and Irish politics, 1926–29

The land annuities, amounting to over £3m per annum, were the mechanism through which Irish farmers repaid the British state, through the Land Commission, for the advances given to them to purchase their farms under the 1891 and 1909 Land Acts. In 1923 the Free State government agreed to collect the annuities and pay them to the British, a commitment confirmed under the Ultimate Financial Settlement of March 1926.[5] The collection of the annuities had been severely disrupted by the War of Independence and Civil War, and it was not until 1925 that the state was in a position to begin collection again. Crucially, arrears had been building since 1919, and it was this that made the annuities such a widespread and punitive financial burden on Irish smallholders in the mid-1920s. Following the signing of the Ultimate Financial Settlement, the drive to collect land annuity arrears was stepped up. By early summer evictions and seizures by bailiffs had begun. O'Donnell denounced the annuities as a 'tax based on the conquest' and asked: 'What district will rush into the van of Ireland's new war?'[6] The answer was provided the following month when he paid a visit to the Rosses.

What *An Phoblacht* described as an 'epidemic of civil bills'[7] were issued to small farmers in the Dungloe district, and O'Donnell was approached by locals for advice on how to respond. He addressed a church gate meeting and had soon organized a small-farmer committee dedicated to resisting annuities, which in the short term meant a campaign of civil disobedience and popular resistance to the bailiffs. On the train back to Dublin, his mind was abuzz as he came to recognize the potential of this nascent agitation:

> Here was what [Fintan] Lalor sighed for: A tax directly payable to Britain: A tax devoid of any vestige of moral sanction. Refuse this tax, have the people take their stand on that refusal, and you faced the government with a challenge it could not refuse and a fight it could not win. Republicans could roast the Treaty in the fire from this kindling. My thoughts raced.[8]

He promised the Rosses committee that *An Phoblacht* 'would pick up every noise they made and make a bugle call of it' so as to spread the agitation. He was true to his word, making the paper 'as near as no matter the official organ of the agitation'.[9] He hoped to build a grass-roots, direct action movement, drawing on the support of republican and labour movements. Despite the support and participation of individual IRA men, the organization never officially came on board. One of O'Donnell's earliest supporters, however, was east Donegal IRA leader Sean McCool, who in September raided the offices of the landlord's agents for the Conyngham Estate in Donegal town, taking away all the records held there. The raid had its desired effect as a temporary morale booster, but it soon proved counter-productive as the Rosses was 'infested' with plain-clothes policemen. O'Donnell, in the meantime, continued to try to spread the agitation, welcoming the beginnings of resistance in Kerry and Wexford and defining the agitation in clear 'national' terms in an attempt to rouse republican support: 'The refusal brings the British bailiff to collect the tribute. The national struggle then rushes to a simple formula. To drive the bailiff from the doorstep. The bailiff's reinforcements are the armed forces of the Empire. The defender of the doorstep rallies to him the people of the nation.'[10]

On 19 February four men were arrested in connection with the raid in Donegal town, one of whom gave evidence against the others.

O'Donnell spoke at a public meeting in support of the men and the local committee capitalized on the publicity and interest generated by the case to formalize itself, drawing up a constitution and membership cards. On 20 March he was arrested in Dublin and charged with conspiring with others to incite tenants to refuse payments of rents and annuities. He was returned for trial on 2 April where he made an impassioned speech about his right and duty to oppose the annuities, stating that he only advised people not to starve in order to pay the annuities. That very week the press had carried reports of the death of a couple, the O'Sullivans, and two of their children from starvation in Adrigole in west Cork, and O'Donnell invoked the case: 'Should the payment of annuities be allowed to cause death by starvation of children?'[11] The republican-feminist Hanna Sheehy Skeffington attended and described the scene in the Irish-American paper *Irish World*:

> [H]e stood there, his face pale, his features clear-cut, his black hair, greying at the temples, his shrewd grey-blue eyes, now lit with kindly humour, now ablaze with passion as he told of the sufferings of his people in Tirconnail. His speech, after the dreary platitudes of the state prosecutor and the hair splitting quibbles of the judge, made a strong impression.[12]

At his full trial the following week, O'Donnell addressed the jury and by all accounts (especially his own!) gave a bravura performance, combining passion, wit and a dash of menace to win them over. He had already made a good impression when, following his refusal to respond to the charges, the jury had to hear evidence to determine whether he was mute by malice or by the visitation of God. As the first juror took his seat, O'Donnell spoke across to him, saying 'Malice, sheer malice', to the amusement of his waiting colleagues. Opening his speech he explained that in not recognizing the court he meant 'the lad in the wig' and not them, whom he regarded as his neighbours. The hint of menace came when he told the jury that the case was part of a continuum of clashes between the state forces and the IRA, and that they should not take sides. He succeeded, against the odds and his own expectations, in persuading them to find him not guilty.[13]

Despite constant harassment and frequent arrests O'Donnell managed to continue writing, both articles for *An Phoblacht* and chapters of his novels, often penned in police custody. Around this time he completed his second book, *Islanders*, which Talbot Press, publishers of *Storm*, wanted to bring out. However, his friend Liam O'Flaherty advised against, denouncing Talbot as 'outrageously vulgar people'.[14] He sent the manuscript to his own mentor, the respected and influential Edward Garnett, a reader for Jonathan Cape, who praised it highly and secured a contract for O'Donnell. 'I am glad you are publishing O'Donnell's book', wrote O'Flaherty:

> he is the coming man in this country . . . you will be quite safe gambling on O'Donnell's future. He is the very best of them here. He is very popular nationally and he has got plenty in him. His experience sounds like a Buffalo Bill serial. He has another novel well on the way, and from what I have read of it it's far more promising than *Islanders*.[15]

The book O'Flaherty was referring to was *Adrigoole*, published by Cape in 1929, which O'Donnell was inspired to write by the Adrigole deaths. Using the actual case, he transferred the setting to his native Donegal with which he was more familiar.[16]

In the meantime, the annuities agitation had managed to push the issue onto the national agenda and in the run-up to the June 1927 general election de Valera said that Fianna Fáil opposed the payment of annuities to England. The characteristic ambiguity in de Valera's statement (wherein he did not urge non-payment, but hinted at retention of the annuities by the Irish state) was an important indicator of the divergent views between himself and O'Donnell on the issue. In an interview in July de Valera stated: 'Our farmers ought certainly to pay something for the privilege of using the land . . . I am not for a repudiation of debt.'[17] O'Donnell likewise believed that farmers should pay something, but not a tax into the capitalist state coffers. His preferred scheme was for the payment of a portion of the sum of the annuities as the basis of an agricultural credit bank controlled by small farmers where money would be loaned at a nominal interest, especially for the facilitation of co-operative ventures.[18]

The election saw Fianna Fáil supplant Sinn Féin, winning forty-four seats, just three short of Cumann na nGaedheal, while Sinn Féin was left with only five. Fianna Fáil was now determined to enter the Free State parliament, and instituted a campaign for a referendum to remove the oath. On 10 July the Minister for Justice, Kevin O'Higgins, was shot dead by republicans in an unauthorized action. The government, linking Fianna Fáil abstentionism to IRA activities, responded with a draconian Public Safety Act and a bill preventing those who refused to take the oath from standing for election. On 11 August Fianna Fáil bit the bullet and entered the Dáil, taking the oath while denouncing it as an empty formula. Cosgrave, now in a minority position, dissolved the Dáil and called another election for 15 September. The results saw increased polarization as both Cumann na nGaedheal and Fianna Fáil gained at the expense of the smaller parties. Sinn Féin were not in a position even to contest the election, and in a transformed political landscape, there was debate in the pages of *An Phoblacht* about the way forward.

Peadar O'Donnell called for a League of Republican Workers, a loose organization of republican activists concentrating on political education and responding to people's struggles, such as that against the annuities. In a series of articles in October–November, he debated the issue with Mary MacSwiney of Sinn Féin. He rejected Sinn Féin's pan-class approach, along with that of Fianna Fáil, declaring that the 'movement for freedom must be based on the peasant farmers and the town workers'. His attitude to Fianna Fáil was that 'what good it does is useful. My method of influencing any organization is to raise issues behind it and force it either to adjust itself so as to ride the tidal wave or get swamped.'[19] He put forward his suggestion for a League at the November 1927 IRA convention, but it was rejected.[20]

By December 1927 the annuities agitation was fifteen months old and stalling. Despite his best efforts, O'Donnell had failed to spread the agitation beyond certain pockets, and even in its heartland of west Donegal it was in danger of collapse in the face of raids, arrests, seizures and a continuing lack of support from the republican and labour movements. Having gone through a temporary crisis, the campaign moved into a new phase in early 1928. Colonel Maurice Moore, a senator who had joined Fianna Fáil, had been speaking out in the Senate about the illegality of the land annuities. O'Donnell had been aware of Moore's opposition, but felt that 'long distance sniping on legal issues offered little shelter for the townlands'.[21] But now Moore arrived at his doorstep with a pamphlet he had produced entitled *British Plunder and Irish Blunder*, which set out the legal and moral case against the annuities; he wanted O'Donnell to serialize it in *An Phoblacht.* O'Donnell could not afford to look this gift horse in the mouth; as he put it later, 'I was desperately in need of some help to widen the area of struggle and to bring new voices on to the land annuity platform.'[22]

Moore had already attempted unsuccessfully to enlist the support of the official labour movement and now O'Donnell attempted to gain trade union support through the Dublin Trades Council. An even more crucial target, however, was Fianna Fáil, and with Moore now on board, O'Donnell decided to 'land it on their lap', despite Sean Lemass having warned him that his party stood to gain from his agitation so long as they could not be accused of having started or promoted it, or of jeopardizing the ownership of property.[23] De Valera had previously banned Fianna Fáil councillors and TDs from appearing on O'Donnell's platforms for this reason.

O'Donnell and Moore began work towards launching a national movement. A major ally at this time was a colourful republican priest based near Loughrea in County Galway, Fr John Fahy, who had organized a group in Galway. Fahy's group had written a 'No Tribute Catechism', which was published in *An Phoblacht*. Some samples convey the flavour: 'Rent is a tribute of slavery enforced by arms by the robber landlords . . . A bailiff is a land robber's assistant . . . a thug and extortioner', etc.[24] A public meeting to launch a national anti-annuities, 'No Tribute' campaign was held in the Rotunda in Dublin on 14 February 1928, presided over by Moore. On the platform were three Fianna Fáil TDs, along with O'Donnell, who said he was speaking on behalf of the representatives of the 'peasant groups' who were in attendance. The meeting passed resolutions declaring the payment of annuities illegal and immoral, and calling for a suspension of decrees, while O'Donnell raised the 'Call off the bailiffs' and 'No Rent' slogans that Fianna Fáil was reticent to endorse. A police report from this time noted:

This Peasants' organisation is the thin end of the Communist wedge. It caters specifically for small farmers who find it difficult to pay their way, and while its 'red' complexion is, for the moment, more or less concealed, it is undoubtedly a movement fraught with great danger to this country.[25]

Its 'red complexion' was to be further diluted from this point on, as Fianna Fáil support coincided with increased moderation, and it was to be two years before O'Donnell reorganized the movement to give it an unconcealed 'red' character.

In the meantime, the Rotunda meeting was followed by others across the country, and O'Donnell devoted his time to travelling the country speaking at meetings. An Anti-Tribute League was formed in July 1928. A key aim was to have county councils pass resolutions against the payment of annuities and for the suspension of decrees.[26] The first success came in Clare in March, on the initiative of Fianna Fáil councillors and campaign supporters, Frank Barrett and Sean Hayes. A major coup was the success in manoeuvring de Valera onto a campaign platform in Ennis, County Clare in June 1928. By the end of the year Galway, Kerry and Leitrim County Councils had joined Clare in passing repudiation resolutions, the Fianna Fáil *árd fheis* had come out against the annuities, while the *Mayo News* and other western papers were offering support to the movement. Yet, on the ground the bailiffs and police were still active (among those jailed were Fr Fahy and Seamus Duirnin, an elderly supporter of O'Donnell's campaign from Croveigh). Fianna Fáil was now at the forefront of the opposition to the annuities, but its position was the most moderate one possible, stressing the Moore line about the illegality of the Ultimate Financial Settlement, arguing not for abolition but retention, and generally sucking the class dimension, so crucial to O'Donnell's conception, from the issue. Once the world recession hit in 1929, the movement became 'self-propelled'. As well as falling agricultural prices, the emigration outlet was cut off and emigrant remittances dwindled, swelling the numbers unable and unwilling to pay annuities. The late 1920s also saw O'Donnell move closer to the communist movement within the context of a strengthening republican-communist nexus, and in 1930 he would help to re-define the anti-annuities agitation in international, communist terms.

O'Donnell and the republican–communist nexus, 1927–29

In the late 1920s the IRA and the communist movement developed links, particularly through cooperation in a number of Comintern front organizations, with O'Donnell as a linchpin. This nexus arose from a combination of factors: the radicalization of the working class and small farmers in the face of the depression; the strategic logic of the tiny communist movement attempting to influence and utilize the far stronger IRA; the Comintern finally abandoning Larkin and reorienting its Irish policy; the high level of shared political analysis between the IRA left and the Irish communists; and the perception by the non-socialist majority of the IRA leadership that it could widen the army's support and recruitment base by creating, or appearing to endorse, a synergy between its militarist project and the growing disenchantment with and opposition to capitalism, nationally and internationally. From the late 1920s to the mid-1930s Peadar O'Donnell's socialist republicanism was to enjoy its most productive and influential period.

Despite the failure to establish a communist party in 1925 because of the antics of Larkin, the Comintern nevertheless retained the belief that he was their main hope for the development of the movement in Ireland until 1929, by which time his IWL was on its last legs. It officially ceased to be the Comintern Irish section in that year and Moscow decided to pursue alternative means of developing communism in Ireland.[27] It now proceeded in two ways: firstly, it brought young Irish cadres for instruction at the Lenin School in Moscow, a key development in the 'russification' or Stalinization of the Irish communist movement, and secondly, it forged links with the IRA, primarily through a number of front organizations. Both of these developments were significant for the story of Irish communism, and also for the politics of Peadar O'Donnell, who worked closely with the communists in these years and was particularly close to Sean Murray, whom he knew since the 1922 IRA convention and who became the dominant figure in the Irish movement in the 1930s. Murray was among the first group to attend the Lenin School from 1928–30.[28]

The first organizational linkages between republicans and the international communist movement in this phase were established in 1927. In February of that year, Frank Ryan and Donal O'Donoghue of the IRA attended the Comintern-organized Congress of Oppressed Nationalities in Brussels, at which a new organization called the League Against Imperialism was formed. The idea was that anti-imperialist and nationalist sentiment in colonial and economically 'backward' countries was the best basis for building communist movements in those areas, with India a particular focus. The League managed to attract a large non-communist membership, including the likes of the African and Indian National Congress parties, but with the shift in Comintern strategy from the 'united front' approach to the sectarian 'class against class' policy in 1928, the LAI became almost exclusively communist.[29]

In 1928 an Irish section was established. Senior IRA men Sean MacBride and Sean MacSwiney were its secretaries and Peadar O'Donnell joined other prominent republicans on the executive.[30] O'Donnell was a constant presence on LAI platforms over the following three years, where the Indian struggle was a dominant theme.[31] The second LAI World Congress was held in Frankfurt on 20–31 July 1929, and O'Donnell accompanied Sean MacBride to represent the Irish section. He addressed a special session on the Irish question. He outlined the history of the Irish struggle and harmonized with the Comintern's recent abandonment of 'stageism' when he ascribed the failure to achieve freedom to adherence to the 'false policy' of 'First of all freedom from British imperialism and after that is gained the social reorganisation.' Furthermore, his criticisms of the Labour Party fitted Moscow's new 'class against class' strategy within which labour reformists were the new enemy number one.[32]

In October 1927 Mick Fitzpatrick of IRA headquarters staff attended
the tenth anniversary celebrations of the Bolshevik revolution in
Moscow and represented Ireland on the presidium of a newly established body that epitomized the Stalinist 'socialism in one country'
approach, the Friends of Soviet Russia (FSR). He began an Irish branch
of that organization in early 1928.[33] In July 1929 another Irish section of
a Comintern organization, the Labour Defence League (ILDL), was
established, featuring communist and IRA figures.[34] It joined another
organization with a strong communist component, the Irish National
Unemployed Movement (INUM), in street demonstrations, strike
support and frequent clashes with the police.[35]

While the IRA leadership had no difficulty in sanctioning the involvement of members in these various groupings, O'Donnell and his allies
on the left were still far from dominant in the organization, though they
were growing in strength, influence and prominence, partly due to the
departure of the de Valera-ites from the leadership. Opposition to the
revolutionary socialists came from a combination of apolitical militarists
and social conservatives. A fourth group, which held the balance of
power, was probably the most representative of majority IRA thinking.
Personified by chief of staff Maurice Twomey, this 'middle group' was
broadly sympathetic to demands for social and economic justice, but
regarded the achievement of national goals as a necessary first step.[36]
They were also pragmatists and 'organization men' who saw that
socialist republicanism offered volunteers 'a deeper rationale for refusing
incorporation in constitutional politics through the blandishments of
Fianna Fáil'.[37] The growing strength of de Valera's party was calling into
question the *raison d'être* of the IRA, while there was an increasing leakage
of volunteers, and especially officers, into Fianna Fáil as it moved towards
power. O'Donnell and his associates provided the IRA, whose membership had dropped from over 20,000 in 1926 to about 5,000 in 1929, with
a political project that differentiated it from Fianna Fáil and fitted the
radical temper of the times. The brief success of the left in swaying this
middle group would lead to the IRA adopting a socialist programme in
1931. At the February 1929 IRA convention O'Donnell put forward a
suggestion for the adoption of a socialist platform, devised by himself and
David Fitzgerald, under the title of 'Saor Éire'. He was supported by the
left, but was opposed by a majority. Twomey and his tendency were still
not convinced and, in the meantime, preferred the safe, anodyne option
of Comhairle na Poblachta, a short-lived attempt at IRA–Sinn Féin political cooperation. Despite its minority position in the organization as a

whole, the left wielded disproportionate influence through its control of propaganda. O'Donnell continued to edit *An Phoblacht* in increasingly difficult circumstances. It was suppressed in late February 1929 and when it reappeared on 18 May, it was under the new editorship of Frank Ryan.[38]

Throughout the spring and summer of 1928 O'Donnell was arrested and released on an almost daily basis. In early June he had what *An Phoblacht* described as 'the unique experience' of being three times arrested and four times unsuccessfully raided within the space of three days.[39] On 28 June Gerald Boland of Fianna Fáil raised the matter in the Dáil, where he accused the state of making 'an unjust and mean attempt' on O'Donnell's life and health.[40] Boland had visited him in custody the previous day and found him in a very weak condition. Thomas Derrig claimed the police had told him that the aim was to break Peadar's health, while de Valera said it appeared to be an attempt to drive out those 'whose only crime is that they love their country'.[41] A week later, following another fruitless police raid on the O'Donnell house, de Valera condemned this 'continuous persecution' and Sean Lemass asked the Minister for Justice how long the 'campaign' would go on.[42] In the circumstances, it is not surprising that O'Donnell decided to leave the country at the end of July for a six-week visit to the US, during which he combined visits to family members and fellow republicans with promotional work for *Islanders*, which had been published in America under the title *The way it was with them*. On his return, the pattern was re-established, and in one fifteen-day period in March 1929 his home was raided without warrant fourteen times.[43]

Frank Ryan was a prominent member of the IRA left, and in many ways a protégé of O'Donnell's. With Geoffrey Coulter and later Hanna Sheehy Skeffington at his side, he maintained the radical editorial line established by O'Donnell in *An Phoblacht*. The paper continued to give publicity and support to the annuities agitation and to the gathering class struggle in urban Ireland, particularly when it involved the activities of what the paper called the 'two wings of the revolutionary movement', the IRA and the communists. The main difference in *An Phoblacht*, besides a new format, was the editorial style; Richard English sums this up well: 'O'Donnell's prose had possessed jovial and witty qualities, with geniality and humour colouring his radical polemicism . . . Ryan was less prone to disguise aggressive attitudes with wit, and his writing elicited fewer smiles than did O'Donnell's.'[44] O'Donnell's presence in the paper was maintained by his regular articles and letters on political matters and in advertisements for, reviews of, and extracts from his novels.

Islanders, Adrigoole and *The Knife*

Islanders, O'Donnell's second novel and his first with Jonathan Cape, was published at the end of 1927.[45] It sold well and received wide critical acclaim in Ireland and abroad. O'Flaherty told a friend in London about the book's 'excellent press', adding that he thought 'it would be a very good thing if the government locked him up for a few years and made him write instead of playing tin soldiers to the danger of the community, and no reasonable good for the spreading of civilization'.[46] After the dubious quality of *Storm*, O'Donnell's literary reputation was established with *Islanders*. It is set in Inniscara, based on Inniskeeragh, and the island, its topography and atmosphere, are beautifully rendered. The key concern, however, is the people of Inniscara, represented by the Doogan family. The short chapters present, in a series of vignettes, the islanders' struggle for survival against the harsh environment, physical and socio-economic. The greater the privations they face, the greater the communal response, while the courage and heroism of these resilient people is portrayed, in different ways, through the characters of the mother, Mary, who eventually gives her life for her family, and her son, Charlie. Neighbourliness, as ever, is the dominant motif and the characterization is brilliantly authentic, achieving O'Donnell's aim of holding a mirror up to the society he is portraying. *An Phoblacht* welcomed O'Donnell to 'the first rank of Irish novelists'; the *New York Times* called it a novel of 'quiet brilliance and power', while the *Spectator* declared *Islanders* 'an intensely beautiful picture of peasant life'.[47] Perhaps the greatest tribute is recounted by the writer Benedict Kiely, who recalled speaking to a man after a lecture he delivered in Iowa in 1968. The man, from Chicago, was blind from birth and had never been to Ireland, yet he revealed a minute knowledge of the landscape of west Donegal and the ways of its people. Kiely was mystified until the man told him that he had read *Islanders* in braille. 'No greater tribute', wrote Kiely, '. . . was ever paid to any novelist than that, over a distance of 5,000 miles he could give sight to the blind.'[48]

O'Donnell's third novel, *Adrigoole*, followed quickly in the summer of 1929. It is by far the gloomiest and most pessimistic of his books, which is not surprising given its inspiration – the deaths from starvation of the O'Sullivans two years previously. His anger is palpable in the depiction of the destruction of Hughie and Brigid Dalach, and their children. The heavy naturalism that pervades the novel, and the universality of its tragic dimension, has dominated literary critiques and has led most commentators to underestimate the importance of the context in which it was written and to misread the political points being made. At the time he wrote it, the author was frustrated at the slow progress of the annuities agitation. His aim was to show the precarious position of small farmers and the fragility of their economy. They could only survive in a context of neighbourliness, and it was the breakdown in this solidarity, primarily caused by the Civil War, that led to the deaths of the Dalachs. At the outset of the annuities agitation in Donegal, he said he was anxious to overcome 'the griosach of bitterness' that smouldered from the Civil War and keen to re-establish 'the pattern of neighbourliness' that had been undermined.[49] His next book, *The Knife* (1930), presented a similar breakdown between certain neighbours, but ended on a positive and optimistic note of the triumph of neighbourliness based on shared class concerns rather than religion. *On the Edge of the Stream* (1934) brought the process a step further in showing how neighbours could progress through establishing a co-operative.

The Dalachs' support for the republicans in the Civil War isolates them in the community. Blight adds to the general problems caused by the poor mountainy bog land of their farm, and demands for rent arrears lead Hughie to work in Scotland where he contracts typhoid fever, further adding to the family's isolation. 'Will neighbours never be neighbours again?', asks Brigid at one stage, as the novel descends into doom. One of the children dies from eating hemlock and Hughie is jailed for a year for his part in a poteen run, but is released after seven months when Brigid and two more of their children are found dead from starvation. The final scene has neighbours gathering nervously, keeping their distance, afraid that it was fever that had killed them. Once the doctor announces that it was hunger, O'Donnell writes, with a bitter irony unique in his work, 'with one impulse neighbourliness flooded warm towards [the house]', as Hughie is taken away to the asylum.[50]

Hanna Sheehy Skeffington was angered by 'the dumb resignation' of the central couple: 'from Hughie and Brigid one would have expected something more upstanding – and from their creator, also, a better moral, for his philosophy is not framed on the lie-down-and-die school of ethics'. Despite her criticisms, she welcomed 'another great Irish novel'.[51] Other reviewers bemoaned its gloominess and lack of humour, but acknowledged its quality.[52] It is certainly the case that, besides his political purpose, O'Donnell is self-consciously stretching himself as a writer in *Adrigoole*, showing confidence in his handling of themes and an expanded range of locations. He has been criticized for the excessive naturalism in the novel,[53] with the mountain, bog and heather existing as hostile, living forces, but those who regard 'Nature versus Man' as the book's main theme miss the central point: it was the breakdown in neighbourliness that allowed the hostile environment to prevail, and it is only through cooperation that poor people like the Dalachs can survive and ultimately prevail. In 1947 Sean O'Faolain paid *Adrigoole* the compliment of including it among only the dozen or so Irish novels he regarded as 'feet-on-the-ground realistic novels', in the esteemed company of the likes of Joyce's *Ulysses*, Edgeworth's *Castlerackrent*, O'Flaherty's *The Informer* and Bowen's *The Last September*.[54]

Republicans were far happier with O'Donnell's next novel, *The Knife*, which was published in the autumn of 1930 and serialized in *An Phoblacht* from December under the heading 'Written of the IRA – For the IRA'.[55] The *Irish Book Lover*, while condemning the book's politics, described its prologue as 'one of the finest pieces of prose written in contemporary Anglo-Irish literature'.[56] The action is set in 'a compact planter district' in the Lagan valley of east Donegal between 1913 and 1923, and examines the crosscurrents of religion, class and nationality in the area against the background of the growth of the independence movement, the War of Independence, partition and Civil War. There is consternation when a Catholic family, the Godfrey Dhus, buy into this Protestant enclave with inherited money. Their 'uppity' behaviour unleashes sectarian tensions and upsets the careful balance developed between the local Orange establishment and the Catholic bourgeoisie. With the coming of the War of Independence and republican counter-government, O'Donnell presents the marginalization of the land struggle and the conservative role of the leadership of Sinn Féin. As in *Adrigoole*, the Treaty split sees neighbourliness torn apart, but an extra dimension is added here with O'Donnell's portrayal of the strength of the neighbourly bond between the local republican and Orange small farmers, which is contrasted with the wilful, bitter and traitorous behaviour of the Free Staters. The book ends with local Orangemen dramatically rescuing the republican, Brian Godfrey Dhu ('The Knife') and the sympathetic Protestant doctor from the clutches of a Free State firing squad.

Alexander Gonzalez regards the book as 'perhaps the weakest piece in the O'Donnell canon', with 'puppets' and 'stereotypes' replacing characters.[57] There is a certain validity to this criticism, as we are presented with a cast of stock characters (the grasping gombeen man, the good Orangeman and the bigoted Orangeman, good republicans and bad Free Staters, etc.), though, as Freyer points out, O'Donnell could probably have cited a prototype for each of them.[58] The most controversial aspect of the book was its treatment of the Catholic Church. In the novel, characters raise objections to the political use of the pulpit to support the Treaty, and bishops are referred to as 'anti-Christs'. The book was attacked from the pulpit, and the *Irish Independent* declared it 'A novel that no Irish Catholic, at any rate, can hope to read without a blush of shame.'[59] Frank Gallagher, editor of the Fianna Fáil paper, the *Irish Press*, who had been in prison at the same time as O'Donnell, claimed that such phrases as used in *The Knife* were never uttered. O'Donnell likened the reaction to the 'Englishman's horror of Irish war books touching the Tan days', and wrote that, in fact, he had understated the level of anger and abuse in the jails.[60] The reaction was partially fuelled by a sense of denial, but it was also very much part of the 'red scare' that was beginning to develop in Ireland at this time, the aim being to establish O'Donnell's anti-clerical credentials as part of a general demonization of the republican–communist nexus.[61]

'A very dangerous individual': from Galway to Berlin

The development of the Catholic Church-led anti-communist crusade during this period was the result of a number of factors: the stepping up of an international campaign against communism led by Pope Pius XI; the boost to Catholic social power in Ireland derived from the huge centenary celebrations of Catholic emancipation in June 1929; the growing strength and profile of communism in Ireland – particularly the 'danger' inherent in the IRA's flirtation with communists and communist ideas. In February 1930, O'Donnell decided to meet head-on the attacks on the Soviet Union being made by Cardinal MacRory. In an open letter, published in *An Phoblacht*, he challenged the notion that there was religious persecution in the Soviet Union. He wrote as 'a humble Catholic' but also as 'a member of the revolutionary working class, and it is in my capacity as such that I meet Your Eminence in your capacity as a champion of the Imperial State'.[62] The letter to MacRory illustrated the extent to which O'Donnell was uncritically endorsing the Soviet line, which is not surprising given that, at this stage, he was operating as a key assistant to the Comintern in building the communist movement in Ireland.

In January 1930, two senior members of the CPGB, Tom Bell and Bob Stewart, arrived in Ireland as Comintern emissaries to prepare the ground for a new communist party. They were assisted by what the Department of Justice described as 'some Irish collaborators, notably, Peadar O'Donnell'.[63] The application of 'class against class' had been delayed in Ireland, and there was a high level of cooperation with republicans in these early preparatory stages. One of Stewart's first tasks was to collaborate with O'Donnell in transforming the Anti-Tribute League into the Irish section of Krestintern, the Peasants' International. Krestintern sought to separate small farmers (also described as peasants or working farmers) from larger farmer interests, and forge them in a revolutionary alliance with agricultural labourers and the urban working class. In 1929 an organizing committee in Berlin began preparations for a European Congress to establish a European Peasants' Committee as the European branch of Krestintern. O'Donnell was contacted and, in January 1930, travelled to Berlin to meet with the committee. On his return, he organized a meeting in Galway on 31 January with delegates from the small farmer committees existing under the Anti-Tribute League umbrella. A provisional organizing committee, with O'Donnell as secretary, was formed, featuring leading members of the annuities agitation. The immediate aim was to organize a national conference and a delegation for the European Congress, fixed for Berlin on 27–30 March. The committee adopted the platform of the European Working Farmers' Organising Committee:

(1) to struggle for the freedom of suppressed nations,
(2) to struggle against landlordism,
(3) against imperialist war,
(4) against exploitation by the banks, trusts, etc.,
(5) against Fascism.

The Irish committee interpreted these slogans to mean, in the Irish context:

(1) the struggle for an independent workers' and small farmers' Republic,
(2) the freeing of the land for usage by working farmers without rent or annuity; the freeing of river fisheries for working fishermen; the distribution of land under control of working farmers in accordance with the needs of agricultural workers; the administration of fisheries by a committee elected by fishers,
(3) opposition to recruitment for the British forces,
(4) resistance to forced sales of cattle and land and to attacks by the banks,
(5) the struggle against the suppression of elected local councils which were championing working farmer rights and the installation of managers in their place by central government.[64]

Over the next month the group, now calling itself the Irish Working Farmers' Committee (IWFC), secured an office at 6 Upper O'Connell Street in Dublin. As O'Donnell worked on organizing the national congress, which was fixed for Galway on 23 March, he and the IWFC office began to occupy a pivotal role in ever-closer communist–republican collaboration, under the ever-watchful eye of the authorities.

On 2, 3 and 5 March a series of meetings were held at 6 Upper O'Connell Street, addressed by Peadar O'Donnell and Bob Stewart, who sought to convince left-leaning volunteers to take up joint membership of the IRA and the embryonic communist party. At a meeting at the same venue on 13 March, O'Donnell and fellow IRA man Patrick Rooney, who had been the manager of *An Phoblacht* during Peadar's editorship, were selected along with Stewart, Bell and a number of Irish communists to form a Preparatory Committee for the formation of a Workers' Revolutionary Party (PCWRP). Weekly meetings were held thereafter, a bookshop was opened on Winetavern Street in Dublin, and O'Donnell (with a brief to cover 'peasant affairs') joined the editorial board of a new weekly paper edited by Bell, the *Workers' Voice*, which was launched on 5 April. While a number of other senior IRA men such as Mick Fitzpatrick were also actively involved at this stage, the authorities saw O'Donnell (described in one report as 'a very dangerous individual') as the most vital link between the IRA and the communists. In a list of seventy-two members of the PCWRP sent by the Gardaí to the Department of Justice in early June 1930, thirty are identified as active IRA men.[65]

On 23 March, O'Donnell arrived in Galway, in the company of Bob Stewart and Sean Hayes, to attend the Irish Working Farmers' Congress. There were forty-three delegates present, representing committees from Galway, Clare, Donegal, Tipperary, Limerick, Longford, Roscommon and Leitrim. In the absence of Eamon Corbett, whose brother had just died, Sean Hayes took the chair. The Congress welcomed the formation in Dublin of the PCWRP, which was presented as the urban equivalent of their own rural revolutionary initiative. Fraternal greetings from the European Peasants' Committee (EPC) were read, and return greetings sent to the European Congress, which was due to gather four days later. The platform and programme of the European Peasants' Congress was accepted, and Fianna Fáil's retention option roundly rejected in favour of a 'No Rent' policy. A key aim was to 'capture' the county councils, push them into the vanguard of the struggle, and make local government, in O'Donnell's words, 'a weapon in the people's hands instead of in their sides'.[66] As mentioned earlier, the IWFC interpreted the defence and extension of county council power as the Irish version of the anti-fascist struggle. O'Donnell was articulating a theme that would re-emerge forcefully during the Republican Congress era of 1934–5: the capturing of county councils and their transformation into workers' and peasants' councils.[67]

His address to the Congress was, as James Hogan might have put it, straight from the Comintern hymnbook. He adapted that organization's priorities to Irish conditions, stressing those indigenous factors most appropriate to the international movement's approach. The provisional committee was strengthened with the addition of representatives from Longford, Leitrim and Roscommon. Eamonn Corbett, Martin Fahy (both of Galway County Council) and Phil MacCauley (O'Donnell's chief lieutenant in the Donegal campaign) were selected as delegates for Berlin and the Irish group joined about one hundred representatives from sixteen other countries there on 27 March. O'Donnell led the delegation and was approached to preside over the opening session, on the basis of Ireland's historical reputation for agrarian struggle and because he was not, officially at least, a communist. According to James Hogan, his opening address saw him 'out-heroding the Herods of the Third International'.[68] The conference lasted three days and heard reports from the countries represented about their respective peasant struggles, while resolutions and pronouncements expressing solidarity with the Soviet Union and committing the conference to the anti-fascist and anti-imperialist struggles were abundant. In his report for the *Workers' Voice*, O'Donnell wrote that it was not a communist conference – 'it is perhaps a pity that it was not. . . . Ah, no, [it] was a congress of peasants.'[69] O'Donnell was elected onto a permanent central committee of twenty-five members, with German communist Harry Richter as president, which in turn elected a secretariat of seven to act as an executive council. Arrangements for the preparation of a bulletin were agreed and the delegates returned home to undertake organizational drives, and were to report back on progress at a follow-up European conference in December.[70]

By this stage, Fianna Fáil was making the running on the annuities issue and its retention demand became the dominant one, despite the efforts of O'Donnell, in alliance with radicals within Fianna Fáil, to push the 'No Rent' and abolition agenda. In the by-election in Longford–Westmeath in June 1930, the Fianna Fáil candidate was victorious in a campaign dominated by the annuities issue. The

IWFC was supposed to be working towards a national congress, but it was July 1931 before two regional conferences were eventually held in Galway and Limerick on the same weekend. In the meantime, the campaign of spreading non-payment, seeking the support of county councillors and resisting seizures continued. The economic depression (which also restricted the emigration option) was beginning to bite in rural and urban Ireland, resulting in the spread of non-payment of annuities and an upsurge in unemployment, unemployed workers' agitation and industrial unrest. The communist-led Irish National Unemployed Movement (INUM) grew rapidly in the early months of 1930 and many of its demonstrations resulted in serious clashes with the police. There was strong IRA rank and file participation in these demonstrations, as volunteers became radicalized by their economic circumstances. O'Donnell led the socialist republicans in increased efforts to pull the IRA into a united front with the embryonic WRP and the IWFC. During the strike of Irish Omnibus Company (IOC) drivers in the summer of 1930, there was evidence of the type of cooperation he envisaged, as the IRA volunteers in Dublin and IWFC activists in Galway, Wexford and Leitrim, took solidarity actions such as shooting at, hijacking and ambushing IOC buses driven by 'scabs'.[71] In the Easter 1930 issue of *An Phoblacht* O'Donnell invoked Connolly, telling volunteers they had to decide whether they were going to be 'the army of the native bourgeoisie . . . [or] the army of the workers'.[72] He argued that the IRA would see its role clearly if Connolly was at the centre of organized workers, but in his absence they should become absorbed in the WRP and play the role of a Connollyite workers' or citizen army. He continued to push this line at public meetings, in the pages of *An Phoblacht* and at PCWRP gatherings in the spring and early summer of 1930.

This approach was undermined when communist tactics changed and 'class against class' was belatedly, gradually and temporarily applied to Ireland. The official labour movement was the first target, but this did not affect relations with left-republicans whose disdain for the labour leadership was rooted in the latter's 'treachery' in supporting the Treaty and Free State. The first evidence of the new communist approach emerged in April 1930 when INUM activists broke up a Labour Party rally against unemployment in Dublin. O'Donnell welcomed the attack on the 'fakers' of the 'Imperial labour party', apparently unaware that the new sectarian policy would soon be applied to republicans. In mid-June the PCRWP was replaced by a reconstituted 'National Committee of the Revolutionary Workers' Party', of which O'Donnell was not a part and which began to push the new line. In the *Workers' Voice* on 28 June an unsigned article presented the 'class against class' line on the IRA, warning volunteers against the treachery of that organisation's leadership: 'Workers who follow Sinn Féin or the IRA are victims of the policy of fraud and deception pursued by the leaders of these organizations.' The new line had arrived in Ireland with the returning cadres from the Lenin School in Moscow, and was outlined in a Comintern document sent back by one of the students, Jim Larkin Jr. The letter outlined the need to differentiate the communists from other radical groupings and win 'the best proletarian elements' of them to the official communist movement. Relations with the republican movement were to be maintained, however, as it still served as 'an avenue of approach to a section of the politically developed peasants, semi-proletarians and even certain proletarian elements'. The aim was a 'united front from below' with the IRA left, while subtly undermining its leadership and stressing the need to absorb it into the communist party.[73]

O'Donnell was taken aback by the *Workers' Voice* article, and concluded that it must have been unsanctioned. He described it as 'disturbing' and attacked the 'unfathomable stupidity' of the editorship for publishing it. He rejected the attack on the IRA leadership as 'sheer treachery to the working class struggle' and stressed to communists that 'the best working class fighters are in the IRA and in the magnetic field of that and the Irish Citizen Army tradition'.[74] The communists, of course, recognized this fact, but wished to win those very 'fighters' from the IRA and bring them into the communist party. In August, the communist William Joss criticized O'Donnell's lack of clarity on the annuities issue, suggesting that his hopes that the annuities issue could be advanced through the existing parties or some form of 'united front' showed that he did not want to 'draw the correct political conclusion which involves the creation of a political party representing the interests of the working farmers and the working class'.[75]

Although relations became strained, and the confrontational and sectarian communist attitude weakened the coalition approach favoured by O'Donnell, there was not the complete breakdown that is sometimes suggested. There was continued joint membership of the IRA and WRP, which continued when the latter became the Revolutionary Workers' Groups (RWG) from November 1930; it was only terminated on IRA orders following the RWG transformation into the Communist Party of Ireland in 1933. Republicans remained prominent in Comintern-linked organizations. The IWFC, as we have seen, remained intact and in June O'Donnell was part of an FSR committee that selected a delegation of eight, mainly republicans, who set off on a visit to the Soviet Union in August. On 24 September *An Phoblacht* editor, Frank Ryan, chaired a League Against Imperialism (LAI) public meeting on India in Dublin attended by 1,200 people. Among the speakers were O'Donnell, Sean Murray (one of the Lenin School returnees) and Indian communist, Krishno Deonarine. Ryan ended the meeting with a call for three cheers for the Workers' Revolutionary Party and the singing of the Red Flag.[76] (In November 1930 the LAI held the first of many Armistice Day-eve demonstrations, which featured what Sean MacBride later described as a 'Republican Who's Who',[77] including Frank Ryan, who was the driving force behind these demonstrations, de Valera and Peadar O'Donnell. From this point on, these Union Jack-burning events became the primary LAI activity in Ireland until it resumed its role as a left republican/communist platform in the new circumstances of 1932–3.)

The new sectarianism (which lasted until the communists realized its counterproductiveness and softened their line from January 1931) put paid to O'Donnell's hopes of a revolutionary partnership of the WRP and a radicalized IRA, and by November 1930 he and his allies had convinced IRA chief of staff, Maurice Twomey, of the need for the IRA itself to take the initiative through the adoption of a socialist programme and the creation of some form of socialist organization to complement the army. By this stage Twomey and the pragmatists were accepting the strategic advantages of presenting a socially radical face as a way of mobilizing support for the IRA, especially as the communists had temporarily withdrawn from their 'partnership' and were offering a counter-attraction to discontented and radicalized volunteers/supporters, or potential volunteers/supporters. In October 1930 David Fitzgerald wrote in *An Phoblacht* of 'the spirit of revolt' and 'active discontentment' amongst the proletariat that had no 'point of focus and no leadership'. Instead of waiting for the people to rally to the IRA, he suggested, 'Why not go to the people?' O'Donnell wrote in November of the need to devise a plan of struggle which would see 'Revolutionary Ireland' capture the county councils and transform them into workers' and peasants' councils, the basis of a revolutionary government.[78] The WRP preparatory committee adopted the new title of Revolutionary Workers' Groups (RWG) in November, the same month that the IRA army council appears to have accepted, for a variety of reasons, the need for a socialistic platform. This eventually took the form a new organization called Saor Éire. It had a slow gestation over the next year, and O'Donnell devoted much attention to it, but, unfortunately for him and the republican left, the IRA's first socialist offspring was destined to be still-born.

Saor Éire

From late November 1930 until February 1931 the pages of *An Phoblacht* became the forum for an open debate and discussion on proposals to redefine the IRA's objectives in socially radical terms. This was a prelude to the February 1931 Army Convention's support of a new constitution for the Irish Republic and the establishment of a new political appendage, Saor Éire.[79] In *An Phoblacht*, in the week before the Convention, O'Donnell warned against a paper organization and stressed that a commitment to a plan of struggle and genuine campaigning activity was needed to make the project a meaningful one for the overthrow of imperialism and capitalism.[80] While O'Donnell and his socialist allies regarded the (socialist) ends as a product of the means of struggle (class struggle), Twomey et al. remained wedded to the notion that once the Republic was achieved, through force of arms, victorious republicans would then impose their new constitution. Their aim was the mobilization of support for the national revolution. Following the endorsement of Saor Éire, O'Donnell threw his weight behind the effort to make it more than a mere rhetorical initiative.

The plan was that the Saor Éire organization would be built on the foundations of IRA units and the working farmer committees. The IWFC experienced a boost at the beginning of 1931 with the publication of Peadar O'Donnell's campaigning pamphlet *Plan of Campaign for Irish Working Farmers*, wherein he pushed the Krestintern/Comintern line about the need for working farmers to break with big farmers, workers from reformist labour leaders, and both groups to combine behind 'revolutionary party leaderships'.[81] The pamphlet had a wide circulation, selling almost 10,000 copies in its first three months. Agitation continued on annuites, forced sales and bank debts, and support for striking sugar beet growers. O'Donnell added the capitalist combines to the landlords and banks in the list of immediate IWFC targets; he called for linkages between the striking farmers and the working farmer committees resisting annuities and sales, and for the increased recruitment of agricultural labourers.[82] An intense period of organizational work in the first half of 1931 had resulted in an IWFC presence in twenty-two of the twenty-six counties, and two conferences were held on the weekend of 5–6 July in Galway and Limerick which updated the platform from the first congress and launched an organizational and agitational drive. O'Donnell combined attendance at local conferences with visits to IRA brigade officers to promote and explain the Saor Éire idea.

A preparatory committee for the Saor Éire National Congress was formed and O'Donnell, Sean MacBride and others on the army council toured the country spreading the message and helping to organize committees to select delegates. There was an increasing overlap between the Saor Éire organizational drive and that of the IWFC. Working farmer meetings were combined with Saor Éire preparatory meetings, giving substance to O'Donnell's aspiration that it be an organization based on IRA units and small farmer committees. In reality, the latter had little structural input and the new 'party' was dependent on IRA structures, which allowed its many opponents at brigade commander level to sabotage preparations. Dan Keating, an IRA veteran from Kerry, remembered O'Donnell coming to the county in the autumn of 1931 and outlining the Saor Éire plan to brigade officers; 'but he made no progress towards converting them', concluded Keating, adding significantly that 'the Army backed Fianna Fáil at the time'.[83] De Valera's party had, in many ways, got there first: numerous Fianna Fáil *cumainn* were in fact transformations of old IRA companies and much of the new party's legendary organizational strength lay in its utilization of existing IRA structures.[84]

While the IRA left was energized by the prospect of Saor Éire, the organization as a whole was displaying what the Department of Justice described as a 'growing audacity and confidence'. An important police agent was executed in January, followed by the killing of a garda superintendent and a witness in an IRA court case in Tipperary in March and July. This was combined with the continuing, and successful, intimidation of jurors and the intensification of drilling exercises. The authorities responded with harassment, arrests and raids.[85] The Easter parades in April 1930 were the largest since the Civil War. O'Donnell addressed the Dublin gathering where he called on revolutionary groups and armed workers to combine in building a 'revolutionary labour movement'. His reference to 'revolutionary groups' of workers was clearly a nod towards the RWG, indicating his continuing belief in a republican–communist alliance.[86] In June, the government banned the annual Wolfe Tone commemoration at Bodenstown on its eve, and the police arrested a number of IRA leaders, including Sean Russell, who was due to deliver the oration. Despite the withdrawal of trains, almost 10,000 people arrived by bus, car, pony and trap and bicycle to defy the ban. Peadar O'Donnell was chosen to deputize for Russell (an anti-political militarist) and delivered a tour de force revolutionary oration. He launched an attack on the 'state machine' in the north and south, which was fulfilling the common task of enforcing the economic conquest. He called for the masses to be brought into revolt against the state across the whole front, and when armed force was needed to break through the military machine, the IRA would surge forward; 'our purpose: to break the connection with England and vest all power in a free Republic in the Irish working class and working farmers'. As Henry Patterson points out, the majority probably missed O'Donnell's intended Connollyite 'identification of the conquest with imposed capitalism and of real freedom with socialism' and saw his speech as an invitation to 'reinterpret concrete social and economic struggles as part of the national struggle'. It was, however, grist to the mill of the conspiracy theorists in the police and Department of Justice, who warned the government that 'One of the principal IRA leaders has recently shown a tendency to adopt the Soviet principle formally as his model.' This period of confidence and radical energy would soon be terminated by government repression, and the ultimate beneficiaries would be the group that O'Donnell noticed at the edge of the great throng as he spoke: de Valera and Fianna Fáil, 'waiting in the wings'.[87]

In July 1931 Sean MacBride was arrested in Kerry in possession of Saor Éire documents. This seems to have been the first clear evidence that the authorities had obtained regarding the IRA's new departure, and provided the police, and commissioner Eoin O'Duffy in particular, with an added string to their bow in their presentation of the subversive threat to the state and demand for draconian powers. In August, the pressure was stepped up with reports to the government on the IRA threat and an extensive memo on the 'Alliance between Irish Republican Army and Communists', a document in which Peadar O'Donnell featured prominently. The adoption of the Saor Éire programme was presented as marking 'the definite union' of the two groups.[88] This document was circulated to the Catholic bishops in mid-September, along with evidence of anti-clericalism in *An Phoblacht* and in *The Knife*. This was a follow-up to a request made by William Cosgrave, President of the Executive Council, to the Catholic primate, Cardinal MacRory, for a joint episcopal statement to coincide with government action against the subversive threat, echoing the combined assault of 1922.[89]

The Saor Éire Congress was held in Dublin on the weekend of 26–27 September 1931 and was chaired by Sean Hayes of the IWFC. There were 120 delegates, together with twenty observers, including Roddy and Nora Connolly. The IRA and Cumann na mBan were strongly represented and formed the majority of the elected executive, which was chaired by Hayes, with Fitzgerald as secretary and O'Donnell a member. The RWG were also present, and one of their number, Nicholas Boran of the Castlecomer miners' group, was elected onto the executive. The Congress adopted a constitution and set of rules, and passed resolutions that were essentially an expansion of the IWFC programme, complete with its slogans ('No Rent!', 'No Forced Sales!', 'Break the Connection with England!', etc.). These formed the basis of a published manifesto, which included predictable attacks on Cumann na nGaedheal and Labour, but more tellingly on Fianna Fáil, the party that Saor Éire was aspiring to overtake and supplant as the political expression of republicanism. Among the ironies of this was the fact that Hayes, as well as being an IRA man, IWFC leader, and now chairman of Saor Éire, was also a Fianna Fáil councillor. Given O'Donnell's centrality to both groups, particularly his propagandist and programme drafting role, the virtually identical terminology and shared aims of Saor Éire and the IWFC are unsurprising. The Saor Éire constitution outlined its objects as:

1. To achieve an independent revolutionary leadership for the working class and working farmers towards the overthrow in Ireland of British Imperialism and its ally, Irish Capitalism.
2. To organize and consolidate the Republic of Ireland on the basis of the possession and administration by the workers and working farmers, of the land, instruments of production, distribution and exchange.
3. To restore and foster the Irish language, culture and games.[90]

Following the congress, Saor Éire headquarters encouraged branches to organize district committees and get the organization up and running. Under the shadow of imminent coercion legislation, which was due to come before the Dáil in mid-October, a series of public meetings were held across the country at which O'Donnell shared Saor Éire platforms with Sean Murray of the RWG and Shapurji Saklatvala of the CPGB.[91] This cooperation throws into question the understanding of Saor Éire as a counter-offensive against the RWG.[92] This attitude may have influenced the thinking of the non-socialists in the IRA leadership, but it was clearly not the position of O'Donnell and the IRA socialists. The RWG obviously feared the challenge of another left-wing organization with a programme remarkably similar to its own, but clearly felt that Saor Éire would falter due to its 'bourgeois' IRA connection; in the meantime, it could offer an improved 'avenue of approach' for the 'real' communists to the politically developed sections of the proletariat and peasantry. In any event, Saor Éire was about to disappear almost as soon as it had begun.

Repression and the red scare

The new coercion legislation, the Constitution Amendment (No. 17) Act, allowing for the insertion of Article 2A into the constitution, was passed on 16 October 1931. It established a military tribunal for political offences, gave the government the power to ban organizations and massively extended police powers. Predictably, Peadar O'Donnell's name cropped up a number of times during the parliamentary debate on the measure, as when the Minister for Justice identified him as a member of the IRA army council when dealing with the connections between Saor Éire and the IRA, and also repeated the Department of Justice error that Peadar had 'chosen' the Irish students to attend the Lenin School. On Sunday 18 October a joint pastoral from the Irish Catholic bishops was read out in all Irish churches. It described Saor Éire as 'frankly Communistic', declared it and the IRA 'sinful and irreligious' and pronounced that no Catholic could lawfully be a member of them. The bishops called for solutions to the country's social and economic problems that were 'in accordance with the traditions of Catholic Ireland', the very solutions that Fianna Fáil was about to offer the electorate.[93] De Valera had reassured MacRory of this at a private meeting, and had reiterated his party's adherence to Catholic principles and rejection of communism during the debates on the coercion legislation.[94]

On 20 October the military tribunal was established and twelve organizations were banned, including the IRA, Saor Éire, the RWG (incorrectly listed as the Workers' Revolutionary Party) and the IWFC. Repression began immediately with arrests, raids and searches, the proclamation of meetings and the repeated confiscation of *An Phoblacht* and *Workers' Voice* until they were forced to discontinue. Within a month, eighteen people were awaiting trial before the military tribunal and those in the IRA leadership who had evaded arrest were in hiding or on the run. The RWG lay low and by mid-December the state had managed to temporarily neutralize all radical opposition.[95] O'Donnell avoided the authorities by staying in a network of safe houses. He also managed to slip out of Ireland, and he and Lile spent Christmas of 1931 in Berlin. During this and other frequent visits to Germany, he witnessed the far more sinister German version of the 'red scare' that had made him a fugitive in Ireland.

During this period of clandestinity, he wrote an account of his Civil War prison experiences, *The Gates Flew Open* (1932) and completed his first and only play, *Wrack* (1933). This tale of poor, island fisher folk was written, he told his publishers, 'in a rage'. He wanted it to be a 'reply' to the bishops' joint pastoral: 'They said Russian Gold was the cause of the unrest. I said such things as the slapping of wet skirts against people's legs. Therefore Wrack.'[96] He managed to pass the script on to W.B. Yeats, director of the Abbey Theatre, and Yeats made 'immediate and elaborate' arrangements for their safe meeting.[97] It was eventually staged in the Abbey in November 1932 to good notices. In the interim, all had changed utterly in Irish politics, and for militant republicans a terrible beauty, in the shape of a Fianna Fáil government, was born.

4

'Bridgeheads of hope'
1932–1939

Cumann na nGaedheal and its supporters continued to fan the flames of the red scare in late 1931, hoping that it would provide enough heat to burn off the political challenge of Fianna Fáil. While the repression had delivered a mortal blow to Saor Éire, driven the communists underground and put a halt to the IRA's gallop, it backfired as the basis of an attack on Fianna Fáil and as an attempt to revive the government's faltering popularity. As O'Donnell himself described it, 'the propagandists said too much. The government arrested too many, too soon . . . The Church-burning, anti-God Reds, when arrested, turned out to be neighbours' sons that grew up among them. Their common sense began to work again.'[1] This 'common sense' was partly expressed in support for Fianna Fáil in the general election called suddenly by the government when it dissolved the Dáil on 29 January 1932.

1932 election

The red scare provided the dynamic of the government's three-week election campaign, as it sought to counter the Fianna Fáil challenge on a platform based on law and order and the communist/subversive threat. Fianna Fáil, however, had been working strenuously since the 1927 election to neutralize the fears of the elites in Irish society, while developing a programme designed to appeal to as broad a constituency as possible. De Valera had managed to reassure the Catholic hierarchy and key elements in the army, Gardaí and Civil Service about the party's reliability. It now offered the electorate a solution to the country's difficulties that was based on 'our own traditional attitude to life, a solution that is Irish and

Catholic'.[2] Fianna Fáil ensured militant republican support by making the repeal of Article 2A and the release of the prisoners a central plank of its platform.[3] The IRA army council suspended the order made at the convention of 1929 forbidding members from election work and voting, and instructed all units to vote against Cumann na nGaedheal.[4] Peadar O'Donnell had proposed that the army put forward a panel of candidates as a way of giving 'coherence to the Fenian radicalism that characterized the crisis' and 'to serve as a rallying point for second tier leadership to impose this militancy on the Fianna Fáil executive'.[5] The army council rejected the proposal ('the bend to "politics" was too sharp', according to Peadar) and O'Donnell believed that the IRA, having already spurned the opportunity to take the leading role in republicanism through engagement in class struggle had now lost even the chance to be in a position to push Fianna Fáil to the left.[6]

While many in the IRA threw their weight behind the Fianna Fáil election effort, O'Donnell lent his name to the campaign of the RWG, which ran Jim Larkin Jr. and Joe Troy in Dublin. He wrote an 'open letter' to Larkin Jr. which was printed as an election leaflet under the heading 'Republican Leader Greets Communist Candidate: Peadar O'Donnell's Message'. The message was pitched at those from small farm backgrounds that were working in Dublin.[7] However many votes his message had won for Larkin, they were insufficient and insignificant. Both he and Troy came bottom of their polls.[8] Fianna Fáil emerged as the largest party and formed a minority government with Labour Party support. It took office on 9 March 1932 in an atmosphere of euphoric expectation. O'Donnell later described it as the 'bright world of 1932, when Cosgrave's Government was smashed, and bitter years of defeat and defamation were avenged . . . "executions" and "excommunications" denounced and disowned'. They were 'days of brave music' when Fianna Fáil's victory promised 'Land, Work, Wages, The Republic'.[9] He was here articulating the expectations of many republicans and the rural and urban poor who had backed de Valera, not those of the IRA left, which had no illusions about Fianna Fáil's role as the party of native capitalism. As George Gilmore put it, 'The important difference between the Fianna Fáil and Cumann na nGaedheal parties lay, not in their leaderships, but in their supporters.'[10]

Giving Fianna Fáil a chance?

There was a sceptical willingness on the part of the majority in the IRA leadership to 'Give Fianna Fáil a Chance'. The new government made a good start by releasing all political prisoners and suspending most of the Article 2A provisions, but de Valera failed to convince the IRA to disband. It grew in morale and strength in the new tolerant atmosphere, but remained politically stalled. 'Boycott British' raids, drills, parades and attacks on Cumann na nGaedheal meetings provided volunteers with a sense of excitement and activity that obscured a lack of political direction. Saor Éire was officially buried at the first post-election Army Convention,[11] symbolizing the beginning of the marginalization of Peadar O'Donnell and his allies as fissures began to appear in the movement united by Cosgrave's repression. 'By all means, give Fianna Fáil a chance', O'Donnell wrote on 2 April, 'to attack the rancher, banker, brewer, sugar combines and other big interests that serve the few and enslave. But don't let this slogan serve as a screen for an attack on the already hard-pressed mass'.[12] He was told by the executive to refrain from criticizing Fianna Fáil, and several of his subsequent articles for *An Phoblacht* were suppressed.[13] His general optimism persisted, however, in contrast to Gilmore, who resigned from the executive (temporarily) and the army council in September 1932, stating:

> I do not agree with Peadar O'Donnell in his belief that there is a revolutionary situation in the country only waiting for someone to assume leadership. On the contrary I believe that practically all the Republican and anti-Free State feeling in the country is hopelessly pro-Dev, and that Fianna Fáil are going to hold the field for some time to come.[14]

In March 1932 Cape had published *The Gates Flew Open*, O'Donnell's account of his Civil War incarceration. The book follows the pattern set in his fiction, with the action presented in episodic form, packed into short chapters. Just as with *The Knife*, the aspect of the book that won it most popular attention, was its account of the prisoners' reaction to the bishops' joint pastoral and the refusal of sacraments by prison chaplains. O'Donnell's 'anti-clericalism' (better described, in P.S. O'Hegarty's phrase, as 'anti-political-priest-ism',[15] or, more accurately, anti-anti-republican-priest-ism!) would soon be in the spotlight again.

In the April 1932 issue of the Dominican magazine, *Irish Rosary*, there appeared an attack on Saor Éire by G.M. Godden, 'A woman', O'Donnell recalled, 'with the sort of shiny eyes that you could mistake for the grace of God made manifest'.[16] She wrote that 'the present directors of Saor Éire include Peadar O'Donnell, who was sent in 1929 with six students to the Lenin College in Moscow to study the technique of revolution', and that the aim of Saor Éire was the establishment of 'an anti-God State'. O'Donnell sued for libel. According to *An Phoblacht*, the decision was a collective one, the aim being to test if the courts, in the new political context, offered a redress for defamation of republicans.[17] As he had never been to Moscow, it seemed that O'Donnell had a strong case. The trial was heard before Justice Hanna and a jury in mid-June 1932, during preparations for the Eucharistic Congress, that huge demonstration of Catholic power that was being held in Dublin the following week. Under questioning from defence counsel, O'Donnell truthfully asserted that he had never been to the Soviet Union and that Saor Éire had not been funded by Moscow gold, but he became more economical with the truth when denying all links with communist and Comintern organizations. The defence case was that the article was fair comment, and the charges true in substance. The supporting evidence was literary and anecdotal. The defence counsel quoted from *The Knife* and *The Gates Flew Open* in building his case for O'Donnell's anti-Catholicism. Lile was called to confirm that he had never been to Russia, followed by the prosecution's star witness, W.B. Yeats, who said the comments would affect O'Donnell's sales, particularly in the US, and had the court in laughter when he said 'he wished Mr O'Donnell would devote his interest entirely to his novels and leave politics for a pastime in old age'. The defence witnesses included a doctor and his son who recalled Peadar telling them he had visited Russia, and Hugh Allen of the Catholic Truth Society who recalled an argument with O'Donnell during which he had said that the greatest mistake they had made in 1922 was that they 'did not shoot every bishop'![18]

Judge Hanna's summing up was hostile to O'Donnell, who he said was obviously associated with all the organizations mentioned. He summed up the issue facing the jury as being whether a charge of 'Sovietism' was defamatory of 'a man like Mr O'Donnell'. He was not a Catholic himself, but said that 'No decent member of any Church would refer to the clergy of his Church in the words that Mr O'Donnell put into the mouths of some of his characters.' He went on to say that there was supposed to be a literary censorship in operation, but some of the passages from *The Knife* would 'disgrace the literature of any Continental country'. Hanna finished by stating that O'Donnell had descended to the level of 'a woman of low position and humble rank, who would be brought before the magistrate and fined 5s for using language that appeared in some of the books'.[19] The jury found that there was no libel, and O'Donnell was ordered to pay substantial costs. A defence fund was established and money poured in to *An Phoblacht* over the following months, not only from republicans, but also from writers, socialists and others who regarded the judgement as flawed and politically motivated. Patrick Carroll, of the Castlecomer miners' group wrote that in 'such an important, politically staged trial the decision must be accepted by every worker as a verdict against his class'. The poet Padraic Colum, despite being an 'unrepentant Cosgravian', lent his support in the belief that 'Irish writers have to stand by each other'.[20]

This same spirit lay behind the formation in September 1932 of the Irish Academy of Letters, a spirit born of the type of hostility to writers and artistic freedom that had revealed itself in the trial. The Academy was the brainchild of Yeats and Shaw, who saw the need for Irish writers to organize in the face of the activities of the newly established Censorship of Publications Board. This body had become operational in 1930 and was already exercising its draconian powers in a manner that left no doubt about its intentions to decimate the literary market in the cause of moral and cultural protectionism. In a letter inviting writers to become members, the two Nobel laureates sought support in forming a body that could represent both the profession and artistic freedom. O'Donnell and Colum were among nineteen leading writers who signed up, along with the likes of Sean O'Faolain, Frank O'Connor and Liam O'Flaherty. The Academy failed to make any impression on the malign growth of literary censorship in Ireland, and did little more than host occasional lectures and give prizes and awards. Despite its political shortcomings, O'Donnell remained an active member over the following decades, and was honorary secretary between 1958 and 1964.[21]

By mid-1932 O'Donnell was 'exhausted from the political struggle' and his thoughts turned to his 'dream of a workshop among fishermen' where he could work on a novel he had in mind. He chose Achill Island in County Mayo, which he had visited in connection with the tatie hokers' strikes in 1918 and 1920. He was friendly with islander Pat McHugh, with whom he and Lile lodged before renting their own cottage. For Peadar O'Donnell to escape politics, however, was simply against nature and, as he said, 'I walked into a Civil War in Achill'.[22] The root issue was agitation for the establishment of a sub-post office in O'Donnell's corner of the island, from where it was a four mile walk to the main post office. The creation of a sub-post office would have altered the pattern of money distribution and social forces on the island, and this, together with O'Donnell's involvement, brought the Vatican and the Soviet Union rapidly into the equation. The parish priest, Fr Campbell, led the campaign against 'Red' O'Donnell, preaching sermons and leading demonstrations to his cottage – 'Faith, Fatherland and the old post office for ever!'[23]

The campaign against the sub-post office was successful, but the efforts to force Peadar and Lile to leave the island failed. There was a strong republican feeling there, people appreciated O'Donnell's (continuing) efforts on behalf of the tatie hokers, while the couple also enjoyed 'the powerful protection' of the McHughs and the McNultys. They gained further respect and appreciation for their help to a local family that had fallen ill with scarlatina. O'Donnell was still in the IRA, of course, and he was involved in drilling and training the young recruits on the island. He enjoyed the social life, and even had stretches of non-political peace and tranquility; 'Neither the Pope nor the Prince of Tides have [sic] written to me for a fortnight', he wrote to his publishers from Achill. 'Roosevelt hasn't consulted me about his troubles. And I'm murdering fish with a net.'[24] He also managed to write one novel, *On the Edge of the Stream* (1934), and completed a pamphlet, *For or Against the Ranchers? Irish Working Farmers in the Economic War* (1932).

The economic war, the land annuities and Irish politics

The 'economic war' with Britain had begun in June–July 1932 when the new Fianna Fáil government withheld the payment of land annuities to Britain, retaining the money instead in the Irish exchequer. The British responded with a tax on Irish imports, which in turn provoked the imposition of tariffs on British imports into Ireland. The 'war' lasted until 1938 and provided both the screen behind which Fianna Fáil pursued its preferred economic strategy, and the backdrop to Irish political developments. The thrust of government agricultural policy was the reorientation of production away from cattle and exports and towards tillage and the home market. Agricultural exports would be used to purchase raw materials for an industrialization drive by native capitalism behind high tariff walls. The large cattle farmers, 'the ranchers', who had benefited most from Cumann na nGaedheal's policies, were now hardest hit, and they and their political representatives campaigned against Fianna Fáil policies and sought the support of small farmers in the name of the threat to the classless 'agricultural community'.

For or Against the Ranchers?, published in October 1932, set out to clarify for small farmers the nature of the rancher position, and to present the situation in imperialist versus nationalist (and, contra Fianna Fáil, revolutionary) terms. It was a clear reassertion, in the new circumstances, of the socialist republican belief in the centrality of class struggle to the republican project. In essence, his argument was that the reliance on cattle exports copperfastened dependence on Britain and thus the imperialist connection. The state must subsidize and enforce a tillage drive funded by taxation of the ranchers and the rich, while releasing small farmers from taxation burdens. Large estates should be taken over by the state and either turned into state farms or be broken up into small-holdings where that was the local demand. This was the way forward in agriculture and would lay the basis for industrialization. That struggle would be led by the small-farmer movement in the countryside in alliance with the working class fighting industrial capitalism in the cities, behind a revolutionary leadership drawn from themselves. This would undo the conquest and pave the way for a workers' and working farmers' republic. This was the line propagated by O'Donnell, together with his socialist republican and communist allies, from LAI platforms in the summer and autumn of 1932. Cumann na nGaedheal described it as 'a plan for Soviets' and tarred Fianna Fáil with the same red brush.[25] The impact of the economic war on cattle exports, and anxiety among large farmers about the nature of Fianna Fáil's tillage plans, radicalized the large farmer sector in a right-wing direction. The former government party was joined by the National Centre Party and the Army Comrades Association (ACA) in opposition to the government from the right, while O'Donnell and the socialist republicans combined with the communists on the left. This ideological polarization would ultimately benefit Fianna Fáil.

The RWG were building towards the launch of a communist party and were increasingly active in the summer and autumn of 1932. O'Donnell, David Fitzgerald and Sean McCool joined Charlotte Despard and four RWG members on the governing committee of the Workers' College, established on Eccles Street in Dublin in November 1932.[26] The College offered lectures and courses on revolutionary and working-class themes, and students were sponsored by political organizations and trade unions. O'Donnell personally sponsored at least one student, Paddy Byrne.[27] Organization of the unemployed in Belfast by the RWG had spectacular results in the autumn of 1932. A series of demonstrations organized by the RWG-led Outdoor Relief Workers' Committee in the late summer and early autumn culminated in a relief workers' strike and mass demonstrations of Protestant and Catholic workers against unemployment in October. There was a police crackdown and serious rioting resulting in the winning of some concessions.

The class unity was hailed by the RWG as a major breakthrough. Both left-wing republicans and communists understandably but mistakenly believed that they had witnessed a major shift in Protestant working-class consciousness. In fact, the brief period of unity was more a product of desperation, and old allegiances soon resurfaced.[28]

The IRA left had hoped that the economic crisis in the North would lead to the breakdown of sectarian politics and, to coincide with the Twelfth of July celebrations in 1932, the army council commissioned O'Donnell to pen an 'An Address from the Army Council of the IRA to the Men and Women of the Orange Order' to be distributed by the IRA in loyalist areas. The address called for class unity against capitalism and imperialism, and assured Protestant workers of a leading role in a new republic based on their 'industrial capacity' and training. The appeal was predictably rejected by the Orange Order and Unionists, while many in the IRA refused to distribute it.[29] The IRA did not participate as an organization in the Outdoor Relief strike and riots, much to the regret of socialist republicans. This confirmed for O'Donnell his view of the Belfast IRA: 'I always maintained and repeatedly said it to the Army Council: "We haven't a battalion of IRA men in Belfast; we just have a battalion of armed Catholics."'[30]

The land annuities issue became live again in the new context of retention and the economic war. The government was now faced with resistance to this 'rent' from the left and the right. The IWFC continued to campaign against payment of the 'tribute' on principle, even if it was retained in Ireland. This resistance was now joined by the strong farmers, who began to default on the basis of the impact on them of the collapse in cattle exports to Britain. Their cause was represented by the National Centre Party and Cumann na nGaedheal, which by the end of the year was calling for remittance. In June 1932 Fianna Fáil had announced a one-year moratorium on defaulting annuities and a suspension of seizures. Peadar O'Donnell claimed that this move was the result of working-farmer agitation within Fianna Fáil *cumainn.* He welcomed the relief, but continued to demand the scrapping of annuities and the Land Commission that collected them. He was glad that his pamphlet on the ranchers had clarified the difference between the two anti-annuity campaigns that had now arisen, and had helped to scupper strong-farmer efforts to recruit working farmers to their campaign.[31] In November 1932 the cabinet received an interesting memorandum from the Department of Finance which warned that the annuities guaranteed land title and that new legislation would be needed if they were scrapped. This would raise the question of land ownership and distribution and

> give point and purpose to the agitation which is being carried on by Peadar O'Donnell's organisation for the non-payment of annuities. It is possible that behind the ostensible object of this organisation there may be a further purpose, that of creating that insecurity of title that would justify the appropriation of all land by the state . . . and the question of land distribution would certainly arise in a revolutionary form.[32]

Cumann na nGaedheal was aware of this dimension, and insisted that the temporary remittance it was demanding be accompanied by a guarantee of title. De Valera, for his part, stressed to farmers that the annuities were the basis of land title and security. He also presented the income from annuities as a means of financing agricultural de-rating (to the primary benefit of large farmers) and land redistribution (to the benefit of small farmers and the landless).[33] Such a cross-class appeal was typical of the successful Fianna Fáil approach.

The IWFC had lost some of its direction and cohesion in the new circumstances, particularly as many activists were Fianna Fáil members and representatives. Existing groups remained active, involved primarily in resistance to forced sales, and new committees were emerging semi-autonomously in various parts of the country. However, at the end of 1932 O'Donnell admitted to the European Peasants' Committee (EPC) that 'it would not be true to say that we have a committee movement at all at the moment'.[34] Committees that arose contacted him and he met their most prominent workers. Often his advice would be sought but he would be asked not to show his face for fear of the 'Communist Scare' being raised. He admitted that most of the agitation occurring was not IWFC-initiated; he wanted to take a back seat, but if the EPC invited Sean Murray to lead a fresh campaign, he would co-operate fully with him: 'He, too, is of small farmer stock and upbringing. His being a communist would be no barrier, for my not being a communist is no asset!'[35]

In January 1933, de Valera called a snap election, hoping to snatch an overall majority before his opponents had time to unite. Cumann na nGaedheal pledged to suspend the payment of annuities for two years and thereafter cut the amount by fifty per cent, a promise echoed by Fianna Fáil. Peadar O'Donnell believed that, in view of the 'various dishonest approaches' to the annuities issue, it was necessary to restate the original case against the payments by putting up an IWFC candidate in the election. He arranged a conference in Dublin where it was decided to run Phil McCauley, O'Donnell's lieutenant since the early days of the campaign, in its original heartland of Donegal. The plan fell through when the group failed to raise the funds and get the nomination through on time. Delegates criticized O'Donnell for not keeping the IWFC alive, and he told them that his desire now was to co-operate with a leadership rather than to lead. The suggestion of Murray taking his place was rejected, and he then agreed to co-operate with a new collective leadership, if such could be organized.[36]

Red scare mongering from the right, and clashes between republicans supporting Fianna Fáil, and the ACA supporting Cumann na nGaedheal and the National Centre Party, marked the election campaign. On the eve of the election, O'Donnell called on small farmers to organize nationally and not allow their needs to become 'a feeding ground for nibbling reformist movements'.[37] Fianna Fáil secured a slender majority, winning seventy-seven seats, a gain of five. Cumann na nGaedheal won forty-eight, a loss of nine, while the Centre Party won eleven, making it the third largest party ahead of Labour, which won eight seats. In March Fianna Fáil announced a further moratorium on annuities payments and reduced by fifty per cent all annuities and rents payable under existing Land Acts.

In 1933 Brian O'Neill, a young scholar, journalist and leading Irish communist, published his book *The War for the Land in Ireland*, a Marxist history of the land struggle. In the introduction, Peadar O'Donnell praised the book for revealing to small farmers 'where exactly the Connolly tradition touches their lives. This book will raise sparks. It may even start a fire.'[38] His optimism, as so often, was misplaced, and his hope that the book would help to revive the small-farmer movement and push it in a revolutionary direction was not borne out. The Comintern's working-farmer movement, both in Ireland and internationally, was on the verge of disintegration. The EPC, along with other Comintern organizations such as the LAI, was forced to abandon Berlin following the coming to power of the Nazis in 1933. Although the secretariat relocated to Amsterdam, the Krestintern was effectively dissolved. In Ireland, O'Donnell admitted by the end of the year, the movement was no more than a collection of 'scattered groups' with himself acting as a 'consulting leadership'.[39] The key task now was the defensive one of resisting the efforts of the right to gain small-farmer backing.

Red scares and Blueshirts

Following the January 1933 election, much of the political heat in Ireland was generated outside of parliament. The IRA stepped up recruitment, the RWG were preparing to launch a communist party and the ACA became increasingly fascistic in action, statement and appearance, adopting the blue shirt as a uniform in March and Nazi-style salutes. Anti-communism developed a fresh dynamic, moving beyond the red scare rhetoric of the clerical and political elites and acquiring a popular resonance and brutality. In County Leitrim a former IRA volunteer and land agitator, Jim Gralton, had returned from New York in 1932 and established a Revolutionary Workers' Group. His political activities and his running of a dance hall in defiance of Church control had made him the target of a clerical campaign. Under pressure from the Bishop of Ardagh and Clonmacnoise, the government issued a deportation order against Gralton in February 1933. He was eligible for deportation as 'an undesirable person' because he was a naturalized American citizen. A campaign against the deportation developed in Dublin and Leitrim.[40] O'Donnell joined a broad-based Gralton Defence Committee in Dublin and spoke against the deportation at a public meeting in Dublin on 27 February, which the IRA leadership had blocked Frank Ryan and Michael Price from attending. The IRA officially condemned the deportation, but was also keen to distance itself from this left-wing cause célèbre. Ironically, Gralton and Peadar did not get on well at a personal level; Gralton once remarked acidly that 'O'Donnell would like to be the bridegroom at every wedding and the corpse at every funeral.'[41] O'Donnell travelled with an RWG entourage from Dublin to Leitrim to hold church gate meetings on 5 March 1933. At Drumsna, the local priest encouraged the congregation to attack O'Donnell as he mounted a ditch to speak. Some local republicans who had had their knuckles rapped by O'Donnell inside the IRA in the past led the assault. O'Donnell told a local reporter that it was the worst attack on him since he was beaten up for being 'a Fenian and a Papist' in Caledon, County Tyrone. The Defence Committee continued its campaign, but to no avail. Gralton was finally caught in August 1933 and deported to the US, where he remained active in communist politics until his death in 1945.[42]

The Gralton episode, and the mob attack on O'Donnell in Leitrim, marked the beginning of a new phase of anti-communist hysteria and activity. At the end of March there was a series of co-ordinated anti-communist attacks in Dublin by mobs that gathered each evening after church services. The RWG had its new headquarters destroyed, and an attack on the Workers' College led to its closure also. The principal organizers were a new group called the St Patrick's Anti-Communist League, which had a strong Blueshirt dimension.[43] The second Communist Party of Ireland (CPI) was eventually launched on 3–4 June 1933 in Dublin. Sean Murray was elected general secretary. It adopted a manifesto centred on the idea that the fight for communism would grow out of the national struggle, and the primary task for communists was to displace Fianna Fáil and the IRA in the leadership of that struggle. Relations with the IRA reached their nadir as the army executive launched a purge against CPI members, and at Bodenstown communists were attacked and had their literature seized. The CPI accused the IRA of sinking to 'the gutter of the anti-communist crusade', a crusade that was gathering momentum with the transformation of the ACA in July into the National Guard, with Eoin O'Duffy as leader. O'Duffy had been sacked as Garda commissioner in February and was now harbouring delusions of becoming a 'green *duce*'. The elimination of the 'communist menace' was the declared primary objective of the Blueshirts, though in reality their target was Fianna Fáil.[44]

The deterioration in IRA–communist relations made Peadar O'Donnell's position even more difficult and marginal, and he and the IRA socialists were temporarily in drift. At the March 1933 Army Convention, a proposal from O'Donnell that the IRA provide active leadership by calling a convention or congress of republicans and radicals from across all organizations was defeated. Furthermore, an order was made forbidding members to promote views not endorsed by the convention. On the basis of this order, the left was 'handcuffed' and 'muzzled' by the leadership. O'Donnell lost his place on the army council, while Frank Ryan resigned as editor of *An Phoblacht* and withdrew from the executive.[45] Meanwhile, Peadar's close ally and collaborator, David Fitzgerald, had fallen ill (and eventually died in September 1933). From his 'back seat' O'Donnell felt increasingly frustrated and powerless as he saw what he regarded as fascism, in the form of the Blueshirts, on the rise with little in the way of co-ordinated popular opposition. He wrote to the EPC on 14 August 1933, the day after the government had banned a planned march on Dublin by the Blueshirts, describing the rising 'fascist menace' that he had witnessed on a tour of the west, and the Blueshirt efforts to gain a standing among small farmers – a prerequisite of fascist success elsewhere. He was critical of Fianna Fáil for using 'the State Machine alone', while the IRA 'continues its private and confidential policy [and] the Labour Party whispers'.[46] The CPI approach was in line with the Comintern 'class against class' policy, whereby reformists and social democrats were regarded as 'social fascists' and the principal enemies – the same lunatic reasoning that opened the path to power for the Nazis in Germany. Peadar intimated in the letter that he and the republican left would have to take the initiative – 'I am afraid I am threatened with a further series of activities!' – an opinion in which his Comintern contacts were 'especially interested'.[47] Just as anti-fascism was becoming the predominant rallying cry of the Comintern, so it became the new point of rally for the republican left in Ireland.

While the communists attempted to co-ordinate anti-fascist action with a 'united front from below' strategy (detaching rank and file republicans and workers from their IRA/Fianna Fáil/Labour leaderships), the popular resistance to the Blueshirts was primarily spontaneous and probably based more on Civil War animosities than on anti-fascist commitment. Throughout late 1933 and early 1934, rank and file IRA activists, militant workers and Fianna Fáil supporters clashed violently with Blueshirts. The government banned the National Guard on 23 August, and reactivated sections of Article 2A, including the military tribunal, before which both Blueshirts and IRA men were charged, thus further distancing Fianna Fáil from the IRA and strengthening its constitutional credentials. In September the Blueshirts merged with Cumann na nGaedheal and the Centre Party to form Fine Gael, with O'Duffy as president. In January 1934 the communists established the Labour League Against Fascism (LLAF) as a vehicle for their 'united front from below', and in February helped to revive the moribund Irish Labour Defence League as another anti-fascist front. A committee was formed with CPI, trade union and INUM members. O'Donnell attended the meeting, but refused a place on the committee because of the difficulty in attending meetings due to his residence on Achill.[48]

The Labour and IRA leaderships held aloof from the street-level struggle against the Blueshirts, both effectively lining up behind Fianna Fáil's state-centred policy. At the IRA Convention of 17 March 1934 a final effort was made by O'Donnell to force the IRA into a radical political role that would build on and offer a lead to the spontaneous anti-Blueshirt activity of the previous six months, and wrest the leadership of republicanism from Fianna Fáil's increasingly tight, moderate grip.

The Republican Congress

Peadar O'Donnell attended his final IRA Army Convention on St Patrick's Day, 1934. He and his allies had been quietly canvassing delegates in advance, hoping, on the basis of dissatisfaction with the leadership's aloofness from the anti-Blueshirt campaign, to garner majority support for a convention or congress of anti-imperialist forces that would free the 'Republican masses' from the 'ball and chain formula of Fianna Fáil'. The first evidence that such a proposal might not succeed came with the rejection of a separate resolution from Michael Price asking for reaffirmation of the IRA's allegiance to a Workers' Republic and a pledge that it would not disband until that was achieved. O'Donnell then put forward his proposal, seconded by Gilmore, which called on the army council to organize for a Republican Congress 'which will restate the whole republican standard and confront the Imperialists with a solid form of Nationalist masses pledged to the achievement of the Republic of Ireland and to the revolutionary struggle in solid association with the IRA.'[49] Although supported by a slim majority of delegates, the vote of the headquarters staff was sufficient to defeat it. O'Donnell and Gilmore, accompanied by Frank Ryan, then left the Convention. Price had already left following the defeat of his proposal.[50]

Their withdrawal from the Convention was followed by their withdrawal from the IRA, but despite this, O'Donnell, Price and Gilmore were suspended by the IRA, awaiting court martial. In the weeks following the Convention O'Donnell and his allies toured the country, meeting supporters and holding discussions with IRA officers, building support for a conference where the next step would be decided. On 7–8 April, former IRA officers, together with leading members of Cumann na mBan and a number of socialists and trade unionists, gathered in Athlone. A manifesto was issued, denouncing capitalism as an obstacle to independence and unity, criticizing the IRA and Fianna Fáil leaderships, and calling for a congress. The IRA army council predictably refuted the criticisms of itself and accused O'Donnell et al. of being 'deserters' whose aim was the disruption of the IRA; it dismissed the congress initiative as constitutionalist – the beginnings of a new political party that would, in time, follow Fianna Fáil into Leinster House.[51]

O'Donnell and Price were tried *in absentia* by a court martial presided over by Sean Russell. They were found guilty of indiscipline and disruption and dismissed 'with ignominy'. A Republican Congress organizing bureau was established in Dublin, made up initially of O'Donnell, Gilmore, Ryan, Price, Nora Connolly O'Brien, and Eithne Coyle and Sighle Humphreys of Cumann na mBan. There followed a series of meetings around the country, including Belfast, at which organizing committees were established. On 5 May a new paper, *Republican Congress*, appeared. O'Donnell was named editor, and edited the first issue, after which Frank Ryan took over as de facto if not nominal editor. The paper sent out the call to all struggling groups to get organized for the Congress: workers, small farmers, fishermen, the unemployed. Special emphasis was given to Belfast workers, who were invited to join the rest of Irish workers in 'the struggle for freedom'. Of all the organizational tasks outlined, the overriding one was the maintenance of a united front through the struggle against fascism; the paper described itself as an organ of that struggle 'above all else'.[52] The momentum built up throughout the summer of 1934 as Congress committees began agitational work. As well as the CPI and its associated groups (INUM, LLAF, ILDL), a range of trade unionists and trade union bodies, including some from Northern Ireland, affiliated or issued supporting calls, including, eventually, the WUI, the presidents of three large unions and the chairs of three trades councils, as well as a range of union officials and rank and file activists. James Connolly Workers' Republican Clubs were established in predominantly loyalist areas of Belfast such as the Shankill Road. The, mainly Protestant, Northern Ireland Socialist Party (NISP) also established Congress branches.

This period from May to September 1934 represented the high point of the socialist republican project in Ireland. The Congress initiative acted as an umbrella and an inspiration for an unprecedented wave of class agitation, organization and struggle, and managed to briefly breach the religious divide in the North and attract organized Protestant workers to a republican banner. The IRA issued an order forbidding members to give support to Congress activities. This led to many defections throughout the country, particularly in Dublin where a large proportion of the brigade went over to the Congress. At Bodenstown in June 1934 the Congress contingent was blocked by the IRA from carrying its banners. Of particular symbolic significance was the attempted seizure of the banners carried by Protestant workers from the Shankill Road in Belfast, with slogans such as 'Break the Connection with Capitalism' and 'United Irishmen of 1934'. Criticism of the IRA actions by O'Donnell and Congress were carefully aimed at the leadership rather than the rank and file.[53]

There was a felt need to create a military wing, if only to satisfy those who were sensitive to the taunts of former IRA comrades that they had abandoned 'the struggle' (synonymous with arms) and were becoming constitutionalists. In July negotiations with the veteran leadership of the moribund Irish Citizen Army resulted in the creation of a new ICA army council, made up of four veterans and four Congress representatives (O'Donnell, Price, Roddy Connolly and Nora Connolly O'Brien). Dublin had the largest ICA companies, given the high level of IRA defections in the city, but there were others across the country, including a large company in Belfast. A number of people wanted to launch a military campaign of assassination and sabotage, but wiser counsels prevailed, and despite continued drilling and training, the focus of Congress activity was open, mass, participatory politics – a unique development in republican history.[54]

The clashes with Blueshirts continued, spearheaded by Congress in Dublin, where it was strongest, and by IRA rank and file elsewhere. Such anti-fascist action was trumpeted by Congress and the CPI, but other factors were more significant in the demise of the, ultimately illusory, 'fascist menace'. The Blueshirts adopted the direct action tactics of O'Donnell's annuities agitation in their campaign against annuities and agricultural rates. The campaign was met with the full force of state repression, and by the end of 1934 had run its course. By September, the leading Fine Gael parliamentarians, together with the Blueshirt theoreticians, James Hogan and Michael Tierney, had tired of O'Duffy and his fascist antics, and he was removed from the leadership. O'Duffy and his followers became isolated as Fine Gael reverted to parliamentary politics. The fascists (or fascistoids) had fatally failed to win the small farmers and the rest of the petty bourgeoisie to their cause, and were over-reliant on strong farmers, a too narrow class base on which to build a successful movement. That class, in any event, gradually came to realize that its fundamental interests were not under fatal threat from Fianna Fáil.

As with other organizations that bore Peadar O'Donnell's stamp during this period – the IWFC and Saor Éire – the Republican Congress promoted the idea of defending and capturing the county councils. Congress regarded the strong-farmer/Blueshirt campaign against rates as a development of the campaign against county councils, aimed at the fascistic destruction of popularly elected bodies, and two Congress candidates were elected in the local elections of May–June 1934. In rural areas, Congress committees campaigned on issues such as land reform and redistribution and the creation of co-operatives. The organization was particularly well organized on the west coast, and O'Donnell's influence ensured a strong branch on Achill. Strikes at the Castlecomer and Arigna mines were supported, and strike support was a major plank of Congress work during that summer. The technique of mass picketing was employed in support of eighteen strikes in 1934, most spectacularly during the strike at O'Mara's Bacon Shops, when almost 200 Congress supporters were arrested and jailed. In late May–early June, 150 unemployed activists staged a 'hunger march', similar to those in Britain and the US, from Cork to Dublin, as part of a series of demonstrations against the Unemployment Assistance Act. Peadar O'Donnell, who assured them of Congress support for their campaign, met them on arrival in Dublin.[55]

While all of these activities helped to make the summer of 1934 a remarkable period for socialist agitation in Ireland, probably the most effective and extensive aspect of Congress activity (in terms of the numbers involved) was its work in relation to the slum housing problem in Irish cities. During this time approximately 90,000 people were living in one-room tenements in Dublin, almost half of which were condemned as unfit for human habitation. Congress activists established Tenant Leagues across Dublin and in the similarly appalling slums of Waterford, Cork and Limerick. *Republican Congress* exposed the reality of living conditions endured by significant numbers of the working class, with accounts by tenants of rat infested, damp, dark and insanitary misery. Petitions demanding better conditions and rent reductions soon developed into rent strikes, which led to evictions, with Congress supporting eviction resistance. In early September, Congress groups in Cork, Dublin and Dun Laoghaire forcibly reinstated tenants evicted after rent strikes, leading to a number of fines and imprisonments. Among those jailed was Cora Hughes, a tireless housing activist whose work in the slums contributed to her contracting TB, from which she later died. Frank Edwards, a local teacher and Congress member, spearheaded the agitation in Waterford, leading to his sacking. Rent strikes won rent reductions in some cases, and rehousing in others, and in general the agitation and exposures forced the realities of the slums onto the national agenda and was influential on the Fianna Fáil slum-clearance programme of the late 1930s and early 1940s.[56]

At the beginning of August, Roddy Connolly (president of Bray Trades Council) failed to convince the Irish Trades Unions Congress (ITUC) to support or affiliate to the Republican Congress, which was due to meet at the end of September 1934. However, those who supported the motion issued two supporting calls: one from eight Northern trade unionists, including William McMullen, the newly elected vice-president of ITUC, and another from sixteen Southern union representatives. In early August also, the continuing poor relations with the IRA led to the withdrawal of the two Cumann na mBan representatives on the organizing bureau, Eithne Coyle and Sighle Humphreys. They had become convinced of the IRA line that the chief aim of Congress was the destruction of the IRA. The bureau was strengthened with the co-option of eight trade unionists, including McMullen, Roddy Connolly, and Barney Conway of the WUI. August also saw four representatives of the Congress form part of the Irish delegation, along with the CPI, to the congress of the Anti-War League, another Comintern creation, in Sheffield.[57]

The Republican Congress finally assembled in Rathmines Town Hall in Dublin on 29–30 September 1934. There were 186 delegates present, representing Congress branches, the CPI and its 'mushroom organizations' (ILDL, LLAF, INUM), the NISP and a number of trade unions and trades councils. There were also fraternal delegates from the international communist movement, including Shapurji Saklatvala, representing the Indian Defence League, Reginald Bridgeman of the LAI, and Max Raylock of the Anti-War League. ITUC vice-president, William McMullen, presided. It soon became apparent that there was a major division of opinion about the form the organization should take and how its (agreed) ultimate objectives would be defined. O'Donnell discovered days before that Price intended to put forward linked policy and organizational resolutions in which a Workers' Republic would be the stated objective and Congress would form itself into a political party. These were supported by a majority of the bureau and thus became the 'majority resolutions'. O'Donnell was horrified by what he later called this 'weird stunt', which seemed a complete misinterpretation of the *raison d'être* of the entire enterprise. He formulated two corresponding 'minority resolutions', proposing a continuation of the 'united front' approach, whereby Congress would be a 'rallying centre for mass struggles' by anti-imperialists of all parties and none, pledged to the realization of 'the Republic', behind a working-class leadership.[58]

O'Donnell argued that the adoption of the Workers' Republic slogan at this stage was premature, a surrender of 'the Republic' to Fianna Fáil, a party that represented the very capitalist interests that stood across the road to its achievement. He argued that it was the nature of the struggle to achieve the Republic that would determine its nature, and one achieved through class struggle 'becomes a Workers' and Small Farmers' Republic because the organs of struggle become the organs of government'.[59] Gilmore and Ryan supported him. The supporters of the Workers' Republic slogan argued on the basis of its clarity in appealing to the working class, north and south. The majority resolution on policy was defeated by ninety-nine votes to eighty-four, after which the linked resolution on organization was withdrawn and the united front approach adopted. Price and Nora Connolly O'Brien then withdrew, bringing almost half the delegates with them, while over half the entire membership subsequently left the organization. Roddy Connolly, despite having been a supporter of the majority resolution, accepted the decision of Congress and remained with it for the time being, though he refused an executive position. O'Donnell (who was chairman), Gilmore and Ryan were joined by Cora Hughes and May Laverty, as well as Sean Murray and Larkin Jr. of the CPI, on the national executive of a much depleted organization.

Accusations that Congress was now little more than a communist front arose from the CPI presence on the executive and the crucial support given to O'Donnell's resolution by delegates from the CPI and its associate organizations. The Communist leader, Sean Murray had spoken strongly against Price's resolution, articulating a version of the 'stages' theory, which contemplated some form of non-socialist or bourgeois stage of independence before the struggle for socialism would commence. As Gilmore pointed out later, both Murray and Price were ignoring the core Connollyite concept of 'the oneness of the struggle for working-class emancipation and for national independence'.[60] O'Donnell's contributions never suggested a bourgeois stage, and were built on the idea of class struggle being the dynamic of the independence movement; his call for the organs of struggle to become the organs of government was certainly not a version of a 'stages' approach. However, his closeness to Murray was doubtless a key influence on him; indeed, Gilmore privately wrote that the Congress idea was the brainchild of Murray and O'Donnell together.

Clearly, the CPI would have had good reason to oppose a new party on self-protective grounds. The united front would allow them to maintain a leading role as a party and to continue the strategy of detaching republicans from petty bourgeois leaders. The communist argument prior to Rathmines had been that the Congress should not define ultimate long-term objectives, but build maximum unity around immediate issues such as opposition to fascism and repression. When faced with the two alternatives, they supported the O'Donnell line, which made the added sense of being in line with the shift in international communist thinking that was occurring at this time. The 'class against class' approach had backfired disastrously and the Soviet Union was now beginning to seek allies in the West against Hitler. This involved diluting the emphasis previously given to the leading role of the Communist Party in any given struggle and the adoption of a Popular Front alliance with any party that would oppose Hitler.

Whatever the actual motivations and influences, the end product of Rathmines was a severely depleted Congress and much bitterness. Its calls for unity had fallen on mostly deaf ears in the mainstream labour and republican movements, and now over half of those who had answered the original call had abandoned it. In *An Phoblacht*, the IRA leadership, awash with *Schadenfreude*, noted, with a satisfying dig at O'Donnell, that the Republican Congress

> took the first steps towards setting up a 'United Front' by splitting . . . [now] its organisers may retire . . . and devote themselves to the organising of peasant conferences in Lithuania or the answering of conundrums such as: when is a Workers' Republic not a Workers' Republic?[61]

Price had declared before leaving the Congress that he was now turning to the Citizen Army. However, this too was to prove problematic as the split spread to the armed wing also.

O'Donnell and Roddy Connolly attempted to hold the ICA for Congress, but the majority of the veteran army council supported the Workers' Republic position and, with Price and Connolly O'Brien, engaged in a bitter, though thankfully unarmed, struggle for control with their opponents. Orders and counter-orders, accusations and counter-accusations were issued in the name of the 'army council' by O'Donnell and Connolly on the one hand, and six of the eight original veteran army council with the support of Price and Connolly O'Brien on the other. The latter group issued a general order on 13 November 1934 ending the fusion with Congress that had taken place in July. The fusion may have been ended, but the confusion had only begun and, amidst the rancour, the Citizen Army fell apart. *Republican Congress* denounced the episode as a 'miserable squabble' and accused Price of a failed attempt to establish a rival army to the IRA, having already failed to establish a party. Price eventually gave up and joined the Labour Party, along with Roddy Connolly, in mid-1935. What remained of the

Republican Congress, meanwhile, forged ahead in its efforts to create the united front, against increasing odds.[62]

United front (on the edge of the stream)

The final months of 1934 saw Congress continue its housing activism, strike support and attacks on the Blueshirts. In November, the Congress/CPI-backed actions of the unemployed movement brought the IRA and mainstream Labour briefly onto a united platform in demonstrations against the Unemployment Assistance Act, while Congress pulled off a symbolic coup by organizing a counter demonstration to the British Legion on Armistice Day, involving 2,000 ex-servicemen.[63] O'Donnell's prison memoir, *The Gates Flew Open*, began serialization in *Republican Congress* in November, but by Christmas the organization had run out of funds and publication of the paper was suspended. It returned as a weekly in April 1935 and was kept afloat for the next eleven months.

Late 1934 also saw the publication of O'Donnell's fifth novel, *On the Edge of the Stream*. Written in Achill, the hymn-singing demonstrations against him there, together with his memories of the conflict around 'The Cope' in the Rosses, provided the inspiration. He set the action in the fictional Donegal townland of Derrymore. Like Pat 'The Cope' Gallagher in 1906, Phil Timony returns from Scotland having been involved in co-operative ventures there and, in the context of growing dissatisfaction with the extortionist behaviour of the local gombeens, organizes a meeting and launches a co-op store. This unleashes a wave of reaction, led by the merchants and the school principal, who push the hapless local priests into the fore of the campaign against this imported socialist 'disease', with often humorous results. This is his most light-hearted novel, a product of the underlying ease of his life in Achill as well as of his bemusement at the burlesque red-baiting he and Lile endured there. A key protagonist is Donal Breslin's 'Government' bull, which is enraged not by a red rag, or even a red flag, but by the St Patrick banner and the drum of the hymn- singing procession of priests, nuns, sodalities and conscripted schoolchildren that made its way past his field to Timony's 'devil possessed cottage'. Having become a townland hero for scattering the procession, the bull falls mysteriously ill and dies. This creates superstitious fears in the locals, which are given a suitable political/diabolical flavour by the missionary priests, brought in by the schoolmaster and the gombeens on the strength of their recent success in whipping up the mobs who destroyed 'Socialist houses' in Dublin.[64] After the climactic mission mass, a mob begins to attack the co-op store, only to turn instead on the gombeen shop when it is revealed by the schoolmaster's wife that the shopkeepers had poisoned the bull.

While the socialist political message is clear throughout the book, Timony is restricted to the role of a catalyst and O'Donnell deliberately avoids the trap of making him a mouthpiece. The central character is not the agitator, but his former sweetheart, Nelly McFadden, whose marriage to Ned Joyce, the school principal, had provoked his leaving for Scotland. The portrayal of her unhappy marriage to the abusive, ignorant and increasingly fascistic Joyce is often superb. The public conflict over the co-op is mirrored in their relationship, as Nelly is empowered along with the community and the tyranny and weakness of Joyce's private patriarchal power is exposed in unison with that of the public power of the capitalists. The dual carriageway to emancipation for Nelly and the broader community is well handled, and climaxes with her precipitating the *volte-face* of the crowd and the public humiliation of her husband and his allies. O'Donnell's fiction had always portrayed strong and resourceful women, but here he is taking a further step with a frankly feminist message.

O'Donnell's next foray into print was a powerful short piece published in the *Irish Press* in reaction to the tragic drowning of nineteen Arranmore islanders on their return journey from the Scottish potato fields in November 1935. In an evocative and angry article, O'Donnell imaginatively described the group's journey from Donegal to Scotland and back, leading up to the tragedy, then: 'Morning. And the world hears. And the world says it was a rock. And the world says: Put up a beacon. And the world says it was a fog . . . but it was not a rock. It was Society. The world has spelled out one of its crimes in corpses.' Sixty years later, the writer Ben Kiely still vividly recalled the impression it made on him: 'That to me was real writing . . . a model of exact brevity, a social history, in little more than a thousand words. In it, the writer and social reformer met in perfect harmony.'[65]

Could Ireland become Communist? The Facts of the Case, by historian, political scientist and erstwhile Blueshirt theoretician, James Hogan, was published in February 1935. It was a detailed red scare tract, which made use of police files to present the danger of communism being introduced to Ireland through the republican movement, and particularly through O'Donnell. Hogan presented the Congress as 'The New Communist Party' and explained how the united front was merely the latest international communist ploy. In later years, O'Donnell, with characteristic modesty, described it as 'a book written about me', and he is indeed a central character.[66] The booklet sold well and was reissued in April 1935, provoking a lively exchange of views in the *Irish Press* in May and early June. Hogan, who in the booklet described O'Donnell as 'a Communist, in the strictest sense of the word, if ever there was one' now called him 'a leading Communist agitator'. O'Donnell responded that he was no more a communist than Liam Mellows and went on to accuse Hogan of being the 'theoretician of Fascism in Ireland'.[67] Both descriptions (or accusations) were comparable in terms of their relative accuracy. Both men, in their own ways, represented hibernicizations of the two ideologies that dominated inter-war Europe. Hogan's political views were, at that time, in broad alignment with the governing ideologies in Mussolini's Italy, Salazar's Portugal and, later, Franco's Spain (though not that of Nazi Germany, which he opposed), just as O'Donnell's were in line with international communism. Hogan (though he did declare in September 1934 that he was 'greatly in favour of the Fascist state') was no more a Fascist 'in the strictest sense of the word' than O'Donnell was a Communist, in the card-carrying sense. A clear difference was that O'Donnell had extensive contacts with the European communist movement, but then, in his eyes, the pursuit of his political project in the Irish context required such support, in contrast to Hogan's right-wing Catholic project, which had a far firmer domestic cultural base upon which to develop.[68]

IRA support for the Dublin tram strike in March–May 1935, during which O'Donnell was arrested together with many other Congress, CPI and IRA activists, was hailed by Congress as evidence of the developing united front. The IRA rejected this framing, however, and the Labour Party and mainstream trade union movement also continued to resist a united front with communists. Communist policy itself was soon to shift, as this period of militancy gave way to the new Popular Front strategy endorsed at the final Comintern Congress in July–August 1935. Communists were now to seek alliances with left- and right-wing social democrats, and even bourgeois parties, so long as they were 'progressive', i.e. were opposed to fascism.[69] In Irish terms this meant, as well as support for reformist labour, a move to 'drag behind the policy of de Valera', as Murray put it in his speech to the Congress.[70] *Republican Congress* ceased publication in February and some months later the Congress offices were vacated. In February, O'Donnell and Ryan had attempted to revive the paper under the title of the *Irish People*, but only a handful of issues appeared.[71] As hopes of class unity in the North went up in smoke with the sectarian riots of the summer of 1935, relations between Fianna Fáil and the IRA continued to deteriorate. The constitutional pursuit of republican goals was slowly yielding results, which, together with 'a judicious combination of jobbery and coercion',[72] was reducing the IRA to insignificance. In an effort to counter its isolation and make itself politically relevant, the IRA, in March 1936, launched a new abstentionist party, Cumann Poblachta na hÉireann. O'Donnell reacted in disgust, recognizing in the move the death throes of his united front dream.[73]

A planned visit by O'Donnell to the Soviet Union some time in 1935 was scuppered by the objections of Harry Pollitt of the CPGB, who was in dispute with O'Donnell about some 'financial transaction'. Sean Murray of the CPI was annoyed, telling the Comintern that O'Donnell,

> despite all his shortcomings, is by no means a person to be despised, and in present circumstances can be of value to our movement. He has a very wide public as a writer both in Ireland and America and has a good record in the Republican movement and is the object of the most violent attack by the Imperialist-clerical reaction because of his Left stand and championship of the United Front and association with us.[74]

More violent attacks were imminent. The Lenten pastorals and mission retreat sermons of early 1936 were again dominated by red scaring. The CPI and Congress contingents were attacked by the 'animal gangs' at the Easter Sunday parade to Glasnevin cemetery, and the following evening a joint Congress/CPI public meeting in College Green ended in violence. The scheduled speakers included Willie Gallacher, the Scottish Communist MP, Peadar O'Donnell and Sean Murray. A crowd of up to 5,000 had gathered, the vast majority of which was hostile. When the platform lorry failed to show, O'Donnell ascended a lamp-post and attempted to address the gathering. He was drowned out by booing and jeering, and soon a fusillade of missiles, including bottles and potatoes studded with razor blades, rained down on him as the crowd surged forward. Believing, according to their own report, his life to be 'in grave danger', the police took O'Donnell into protective custody.[75]

The IRA had committed two high-profile murders in March and April, and in May chief of staff, Maurice Twomey, was arrested. On 18 June the IRA was declared illegal and the Bodenstown commemoration was banned. The following day, Twomey was sentenced to three years imprisonment and the IRA leadership went into hiding. *An Phoblacht* was suppressed in early July and the *Workers' Voice* folded in June. In the Dublin Corporation elections at the end of the month Congress candidates Gilmore and Ryan performed pitiably, while the CPI withdrew its candidates in favour of the Labour Party. With his socialist republican project in tatters, the united front as far away as ever, and bottles breaking over his head, Peadar O'Donnell made an understandable decision: 'I decided to search out a fishing village in Scotland . . . There was a touch of edging away from cross dogs in my search for a cottage in the Highlands; crowds had got into the habit of singing hymns at me and hurling bottles. But I missed the turn for Scotland and took the road to Spain instead.'[76] True to his pattern hitherto, he was going from the frying pan into the fire.

Salud! An Irishman and the Spanish Civil War

The O'Donnells had been considering seeking refuge in Scotland when some friends announced that they were taking a holiday in Spain, so they decided to accompany them in the hope of finding that elusive 'workshop among fishermen'. They departed in early July 1936 for the Catalonian fishing village of Sitges, thirty miles from Barcelona. O'Donnell's main ambition was to finish a half-started novel, though en route he also began thinking about a booklet on the changed agrarian situation in Spain since the centre-left Popular Front government had come to power in February. Events would soon overtake both objectives.[77]

Based in Sitges, O'Donnell travelled frequently to Barcelona. He sought out contacts in the Communist Party, which he assumed represented the main working-class grouping, but soon discovered that the anarchists and anarcho-syndicalists, organized in the FAI (political organization) and the CNT (trade union), were the most powerful force, while the communists had hardly a presence. He arranged a meeting with the anarchists, was warmly welcomed and invited to attend planned regional conferences on rural collectivization. On 17 July Franco and 'the generals' launched their rising against the government, with the backing of the Spanish elites, Fascist Italy and Nazi Germany. The rising was crushed in Barcelona and Madrid by the working-class organizations, and sparked a social revolution in many parts of Spain. The O'Donnells secured permits and travelled to Barcelona, the epicentre of the revolution, with a group of anarchist militia men.[78] The city was awash with revolutionary excitement and they wandered the packed streets absorbing the atmosphere and marvelling at 'that cityful of people, who preserved such uncanny order even in this first flush of their victory'. The following day O'Donnell was brought on board to edit the English language version of the anarchists' international news bulletin and was given a press pass endorsed by the new Anti-Fascist Militia Committee. The couple accompanied the first militias from Barcelona to leave for the Aragon Front, carried along by the collective passion and energy. They returned after a few days to 'queer, tangled Barcelona, knitting together its new life', with the workers 'in the first flush of their overlordship of industries'. Encouraged by their friends, they decided that the best contribution they could now make was to return to Ireland to present an eyewitness account of events in Spain. The 'dream workshop' and the books O'Donnell hoped would come from it had become early casualties of the Spanish Civil War.[79]

The outbreak of the war sparked a resurgence of the ideological and cultural battles that had characterized Irish politics in the preceding years. The Blueshirt elements came to the fore; Paddy Belton led the Irish Christian Front, the main pro-Franco political campaign, and Eoin O'Duffy organized an Irish Brigade to carry his crusade to Spain. The *Irish Independent* newspaper, the Catholic Church, and the Fine Gael party formed a powerful pro-Franco bloc; the Labour Party cowered and the Fianna Fáil government maintained an officially neutral stance, falling in with the 'non-intervention' position of the western democracies. Support for the Spanish republic came from the Republican Congress, the CPI and a scattering of independent socialists and republicans.[80] Spain provided a focus for the attempted revival of the united front, and it brought Congress back to life and into ever closer association with the CPI. The latter took the Stalinist Popular Front line on Spain whereby bourgeois democracy, and not socialist revolution, was presented as the bulwark against fascism. Peadar O'Donnell and Congress supporters largely followed the CPI line on the war.

From the outset, the Irish public was bombarded with atrocity story propaganda from Spain, dominated by false, exaggerated and decontextualized reports of attacks on priests, nuns and churches. The central issue (a fascist-backed military rising against an elected government) was lost and the conflict was presented as a battle between godless reds on one side and the forces of Christianity on the other. The countering of this propaganda provided the focus of pro-republican activities in the opening months of the war, and O'Donnell was a crucial contributor, given his direct experiences. In newspaper interviews and public meetings in August, he described the popular nature of the response to the rising and countered the propaganda about church burning.[81] The origins of the rising in Morocco and the presence of a large contingent of Moors and foreign legionnaires in Franco's forces was seized upon by the Irish left to undermine the presentation of the conflict in pro- and anti-Christian terms. O'Donnell presented the war as 'a fight of the poor against the rich, of the people against the landlords, of a Democratic government against a military junta, and finally, of the Catholic masses against the Moors and the Foreign Legion'.[82] This line was echoed in the pages of the CPI's *The Worker* and was a key component of the Republican Congress campaign. In an article on Spain in *Ireland To-day* in September 1936, O'Donnell opens by pointing out the irony that he and the communists not only were lone voices supporting bourgeois democracy, but were alone in acclaiming 'Catholic Spain against the Moors and Legionnaires'. He refers to reports of the Badajoz massacre of 2,000 Catholic workers by Moors, which made 'some of our principal Irish newspapers . . . publicists for the heathen, while this group of ours is for the Catholic masses'.[83] This approach was reflected in the disproportionate coverage in pro-republican articles and speeches given to anti-Franco Catholics like Fr Michael O'Flanagan and the Basque priest, Fr Laborda, who visited Ireland in early 1937.

O'Donnell returned to Spain at the beginning of September 1936 and addressed the large peasants' conference that was held in Barcelona on 5 September. 'I was sorely tempted', he wrote, 'to send telegrams to a few outstanding reactionary farmers in Ireland to tell them that I would have much pleasure in conveying their greetings to the Anarchist Farmers' Congress.'[84] He devotes a whole chapter of his book on his time in Spain, *Salud! An Irishman in Spain* (1937), to this congress, indicating, as does his reproduction of the decrees issued by industrial syndicates, his concern to document the revolution as it was happening. His account of the speeches and contributions, centring on the pace of collectivization, reflects his own views arising from his Irish experience, where the large numbers of smallholders was similar to Catalonia. He instinctively sided with those who argued for partial, staged collectivization. Compromise was reached to allow those with small farms to continue to work them with family labour, while derelict farms and those of the enemy were to be collectivized, and no rents were to be paid to landlords. The acknowledgement of the universal peasant 'passion for a piece of land' was, for O'Donnell, a victory for common sense, and highlights his pragmatic approach to the land question: strive for the collective ideal while allowing room for individualization. The small farmer, he wrote in 1930, was 'wedged into his holding . . . [G]uaranteed tenure of the working farmer must continue, for it is that ease and rest of mind that will enable his thoughts to ripen for collective effort.'[85]

He set off for Madrid and immediately noted the communist influence, in contrast with Barcelona where the anarchists were the driving force. He believed this to be an instinctive reaction to the fascist attacks on communism: 'If Communism was the enemy-in-chief in the eyes of the Fascists then it clearly was a fighting formation to which anti-Fascists should rally. There was also a groping hope of help from the Soviet Union . . .'. He found that Madrid did not give 'that impression of a people set free which Barcelona did'. In discussions with foreigners and Spaniards in Madrid he heard again 'this distant-minded judgement of the Anarchists. There was some surprise at my enthusiasm for them, for it was taken for granted that every foreigner coming to Madrid at this stage was a Communist.'[86]

During a discussion with an official at the British consulate, he was told the story of the Duchess of Tetuan. Her name was O'Donnell, a descendant of a branch of the Donegal family that had fled to Spain in the seventeenth century. Her father had been Minister for War in the dictatorship of Primo Rivera, which collapsed in 1931. She had an apartment in a building she owned in Madrid that also housed the Irish consulate. Following the outbreak of the war, the Irish legation transferred out of Madrid, and the Duchess, fearing for her safety, had put the consulate notice on her own door in an effort at protection. O'Donnell, declaring himself 'a bigoted Tir Conaillian', decided he had to do what he could for this fascist sympathizer, who was now under house arrest. He managed to secure a meeting with the republican Minister for Foreign Affairs, who assured him that beyond arrest, nothing more would be done to her. Further lobbying secured the Duchess safe passage out of the republican zone. As we shall see, this seemingly bizarre investment of time and energy paid some dividends two years later.[87] His final impressions of Spain were of increasing communist influence in the republican zone, and with the International Brigades arriving and the defence of Madrid beginning, he made his way back to Ireland.

At home, he found the battle for public opinion 'rather one-sided'. Irish republicans 'sulked' in the face of the simplified presentation of the war and adopted the position that 'they were not favouring or fighting alongside people who led the war against our own Republic in 1922–3'.[88] The communists were undertaking the task assigned to communist parties everywhere and were recruiting for the International

Brigades. O'Donnell and others in Congress were initially lukewarm about the idea of losing the few activists they had to Spain. Once O'Duffy's brigade set off in November, many young activists, predominantly from Congress but also a number from the IRA, were motivated to continue the anti-Blueshirt fight in Spain. The first group of eighty set off in December under the leadership of Frank Ryan. Eventually some 200 Irish people fought with the Brigades in Spain, including many of those who had formed the core of Congress. Approximately one third were killed and many more never returned to Ireland.[89] O'Donnell was 'full of Spain'[90] on his return and he launched himself into the support campaign that was developing in Ireland. He joined in the work of the pro-republican committees such as the Spanish Medical Relief Committee and the Spanish Aid Committee. The CPI and Congress failed to mobilize the united front they had hoped for, and had to be satisfied with the support of individuals like Fr O'Flanagan, Owen Sheehy Skeffington and Ernie O'Malley. The latter chaired a large public meeting in November 1936 in Dublin, aimed at rallying Irish republican opinion, at which O'Donnell focused his attack on the media *bête noire* of Irish republicans, the *Irish Independent*. In January 1937 he shared platforms with anti-Franco Basque priest, Fr Ramon Laborda, invited to Ireland by George Gilmore. Laborda had attended the 1932 Eucharistic Congress as part of the Spanish delegation, and so had strong credentials. Despite causing some 'embarrassment to the Government', he made little dent on public opinion, either in January or when he returned the following month.[91]

In March 1937 the CPI, Congress and the NISP joined forces to launch a new weekly paper, the *Irish Democrat*, which ran until the end of the year. Spain provided the main focus, and O'Donnell contributed a 'Weekly Commentary', which ran until June. He did not take the task too seriously, and his columns were little more than light-hearted miscellanies. He did not engage with the Spanish question and kept quiet about his self-described 'enthusiasm' for the anarchists and the social revolution that he had witnessed. The communist position, to which he had clearly chosen to defer, was hostile to the revolution that was taking place in conjunction with the Civil War, and particularly hostile to the POUM (Workers' Party of Marxist Unity), the anti-Stalinist socialist party/militia that was allied to the anarchists. In May 1937, the Spanish communists – who had gained a dominant position due to the Soviet Union being the only state supporter of the republican fight – assisted by Stalin's secret police, led an assault on the revolutionary workers in

Barcelona. Popular Front strategy required the crushing of socialist revolution, which the anarchists and the POUM regarded as the core of the anti-fascist struggle, in the cause of defending bourgeois democracy and fulfilling Stalin's foreign policy requirements. Voicing the communist line, Frank Ryan wrote articles in the *Irish Democrat* in May describing the POUM as 'a Fascist force in the rear'. The NISP, which supported the POUM, withdrew from the paper in protest. O'Donnell did not take a public position on this issue, though when *Salud!* was published, his attitude at the time of writing it was clear. The review of the book in the *Democrat* made no reference to his enthusiasm for the revolution, though in a letter from Spain to Sean Murray in September 1937, Ryan made reference to 'Peadar's friends (the Anarchists)'. In general, the attitude of Irish communists and Brigadiers was to regard the anarchists as generally sincere, if hapless, undisciplined and misguided, while the POUM was regarded as a fascist agent; its real sin, of course, was to be a Marxist organization that rejected the authority of the Comintern and the Stalinist monopolization of communist politics worldwide.[92] *Salud!* was published in May 1937. There are some brilliant descriptive passages and examples of what Gonzalez calls 'camera-eye realism', but overall the impression is of a hastily composed book, rushed out as a contribution to the debate on Spain in Ireland and Britain. The *Irish Book Lover*, while acknowledging 'passages of real genius' and 'Peadar's eminently readable style', takes issue with '[o]ur author's interest in the Anarchists', which, it concludes, 'can only be excused by his well-known sympathy with the landless and small farmers everywhere.'[93]

The gradual decline of the pro-republican campaign in Ireland, in a context of continuing hostility and increasing apathy, was marked by the demise of the *Democrat* in December 1937. There was a shift in attention from political concerns to humanitarian activities with the establishment in 1938 of the Food Ship for Spain Committee, which gathered relief supplies, and the broadly-supported Frank Ryan Release Committee, of which O'Donnell was a member. Ryan had been captured in 1938 and was incarcerated at Burgos prison. One of those who took up his cause was the Duchess of Tetuan, in return for O'Donnell's efforts on her behalf in 1936. She visited Ryan and used her contacts with the Francoists to lobby for his release.[94] In July 1940, Ryan was allowed to 'escape' into the hands of the Germans by the new Franco government, which had won the Civil War in March 1939. The Nazis hoped he might be of use in their wartime efforts to mobilize Irish republican opinion against Britain. He eventually died in Dresden in 1944.

The Spanish Civil War was the 'last hurrah' of the Irish interwar socialist republican movement. Frank Edwards recalled the changed situation that met him on his return from Spain: 'The Christian Front was gone, so too were the last fragments of Republican Congress. All my old friends were retired to the sidelines. No political organization existed in which they could play a part.' The loss of activists and leaders of the calibre of Charlie Donnelly and Frank Ryan was not something such a tiny movement could afford. Nevertheless, the movement was already in terminal decline in 1936, and one interpretation of the exodus to Spain is that it represented an implicit admission of frustration and defeat at home. Eugene Downing of the CPI, who went in 1938, described it as 'a kind of lifeline for frustrated left-wingers. This is something we can do. This is where the battle is being fought.' Peadar O'Donnell was of the opinion that 'the left's losses in the war did not hurt it decisively. It had already been weakened.'[95]

The constitution, the bothy fire 'and all that'

In May 1937 the Irish government published the draft of a new constitution that would be put to the people in a referendum in July. The new constitution was intended to represent another landmark on the road to Irish sovereignty, and the legitimization of the state in the face of the IRA. The document encapsulated and reflected the dominant Catholic nationalist ethos in the state, but refrained from declaring a republic because of the continuance of partition. The 'natural' right to private property was enshrined, divorce was prohibited, and a woman's place was declared to be 'in the home'. The most vocal radical opposition came from a small number of feminist groups and prominent liberal women, but the non-Fianna Fáil republicans also rejected the constitution, mainly on the grounds that it implicitly recognized partition. *An Phoblacht* was revived for six issues from mid-May and issued an invitation to all organizations and individuals who were opposed to 'this sham document' to send in statements and articles. O'Donnell's contribution condemned it for copperfastening partition by creating a southern Catholic state to match the northern Protestant one. He believed a republic should be declared and a nationwide conference called to push for unity. Discussions were held about calling such a conference, but nothing came of it. In a joint statement in the *Irish Democrat*, O'Donnell and Frank Ryan raised the religious issue again, but also the gender and class dimension. They contrasted it with the egalitarianism of the 1916 Proclamation, pointing out that 'equal pay and opportunities for women' should be a central part of any republican constitution, and condemning the raising of private property to 'the dignity of a sacrament'.[96] The constitution was passed by a narrow majority and de Valera could now claim a new legitimacy, while the IRA was at a low ebb, divided and marginalized. The apolitical militarist, Sean Russell, who had been planning a bombing campaign in Britain, became chief of staff and his supporters captured the leadership.[97] In April 1938 the Anglo-Irish Agreement ended the economic war and secured the return of the Treaty ports, which, together with the constitution, laid the basis for Irish neutrality in the upcoming war.

Meanwhile, on 16 September 1937, ten young Achill islanders died in Kirkintolloch, Dumbartonshire, Scotland when the bothy in which they were sleeping burnt down. The victims were mainly young teenagers. The tragedy, coming as it did on the heels of the Arranmore tragedy of 1935, provoked sadness followed by anger in the migratory areas of the west. Peadar O'Donnell felt the call to action. While the government shed crocodile tears and established a commission to look into the question of migratory workers, O'Donnell set out for the west to help organize the workers themselves. He worked to form an Irish migratory workers' branch of the Scottish Farm Servants' Union (now a section of the Transport Union). He travelled to Scotland for the beginning of the picking season in June 1938 to help in registering the arriving Irish workers in the union, but, despite the best efforts of O'Donnell and his colleagues, few workers joined, reluctant to pay the dues and intimidated by the 'gaffers'. Nevertheless, the core that had organized represented for O'Donnell the vanguard for the future.[98]

In November–December 1937, while the meetings to organize the workers were beginning in Achill, O'Donnell published a pamphlet entitled *The Bothy Fire and All That*. As well as a tract inspired by the inconclusive report of the inquiry into the fire, it included a reprint of his article on the Arranmore disaster. His piece on the bothy fire is predominantly an analysis of the failure, and inability, of the Fianna Fáil government to deliver on its promises, and a rallying call to the rural poor, who needed to be 'startled into a sense of their own stature'. The pamphlet is full of detailed plans to save the west, based on the break up of ranches and an increased role by the state: state farms and the development of the peat bogs in the midlands, leading to new co-operative villages. These should be the type of demands made by the beleaguered people of the west, organized into committees to force the government into action, backed by the working class who would gain by the development of industry, and republican groups for whom such a development would represent a contribution to the struggle against imperialism. He described it all as 'the struggle to complete the National revolution which de Valera and his manufacturers cannot complete', 'this middle class revolution', and an 'advance within the boundaries of capitalism'. He retained the belief in the possibility of such a campaign becoming revolutionary, if it was led by the trade unions, together with the 'rural battalions' and 'Republican and Democratic forces', but was primarily contemplating and advocating a push on de Valera and the native bourgeoisie to offer a solution, resulting in a 'thickening of the defences of capitalism' but also a 'vastly strengthened working class to face the job ahead'.[99] This articulation of a version of the communist 'stages theory', albeit with a strong radical and practical undercurrent, marks a key, if subtle shift in O'Donnell's political position.

The failure of the migratory workers to organize over the following year symbolized the hopelessness of bringing O'Donnell's proposals to even partial realization. Fianna Fáil policy was actually moving, or continuing to move, in the opposite direction to that which he envisaged. Land division was abandoned after 1935 and the logic of the cattle economy was accepted, which meant a de facto acceptance of the inevitability of continuing rural depopulation and the economic and demographic decline of the small-farm countryside. The government minimized rather than maximized state involvement in the economy and continued to base its developmental strategy on the 'economic leadership of the national bourgeoisie'. Its financial dependency on business interests grew, and the party increasingly attracted, and became electorally dependent on, the majority of the urban working class and the industrial and commercial bourgeoisie. Welfare concessions (what O'Donnell derisively called 'free meat and pocket money'), price supports and subsidies established dependency on the party and a sufficient level of electoral loyalty to it among small farmers.[100] The discontent in the west with Fianna Fáil policies found brief political expression in the 1940s through Clann na Talmhan, a party founded in 1938 to represent the interests of small farmers, which, despite its radical rhetoric, turned out to be essentially a conservative party of protest. Over two decades would pass before a 'Save the West' campaign, based on local, community development initiatives of the type O'Donnell advocated in the late 1930s, would emerge. He was again at its centre, and it would again perish, this time on the rocks of Fianna Fáil's new developmental strategy based on international capital.

In the summer of 1939, Peadar O'Donnell and Lile set off for a long holiday in the United States. In New York, wearing his writer's hat, he addressed a series of meetings on Irish themes, organized by the 'Irish Writers Discussion Group'. This was, according to one critic, 'a fictitious and paper body' used as a front by two CPUSA members who organized the meetings.[101] Pat Quinlan, an Irish-American who had worked with James Connolly in the American Socialist Party, in an article in the *Gaelic American*, launched an attack on O'Donnell, describing him as a 'fellow traveller' of the Communist Party who was careful to follow their line by avoiding criticisms of de Valera and the British (who were potential allies of the Soviet Union until the Hitler–Stalin pact of August 1939). O'Donnell responded, declaring that, despite his being labelled a communist by all and sundry, 'the Communist Party of Ireland have stubbornly denied me the status'. He explained his comments about Ireland being 'a better land to-day': 'I am not thinking of parties, nor the Free State, nor Éire, but of new flashes in the people themselves.' He went on to write of the new energy abroad in rural Ireland since the bothy fire, and how 'a knowledge of Connolly would resolve confusion in the awakening people', particularly the 'Catholic Connolly' who, in his American debates with the socialist leader De Leon, took 'a stand against the invasion of the essentials of the working class struggle with ideas objectionable to Catholics . . . the answer to every Catholic hesitation is to be found in the stand taken by Connolly.'[102]

It is likely that it was while moving in American communist circles at this time that O'Donnell met Paul Robeson, the famous black American singer and actor, who was a party member. However, according to legend (which always offers a better story), Peadar was stranded at a roadside with a burst tyre when a limousine stopped and offered help. He was invited to sit in the car by the passenger while the driver fixed the puncture. The passenger turned out to be Robeson, who told Peadar he would like to record an Irish song. O'Donnell suggested *Kevin Barry*, the ballad glorifying the young IRA man hanged by the British in 1920, which he said conveyed the spirit of Ireland. He proceeded to teach the song to Robeson, who released it on record in the early 1950s.[103]

Personal tragedy also struck on that eventful trip when in August his brother Joe was killed in an accident in New York. Peadar and Lile offered to take Joe's son Peter (Peadar Joe), who was nearing his fifth birthday, back to Ireland with them on an extended holiday. When the Second World War broke out in September, it was decided that he would remain for the duration, and it developed into a permanent arrangement whereby the couple unofficially adopted the boy, who they reared as a son. This new addition obviously transformed their private lives, but it is possible that it also influenced O'Donnell's participation in public life, as we will see. November 1939 brought the death of his old friend, Charlotte Despard, the feminist, socialist and republican. Her coffin was carried into Glasnevin cemetery by the playwright Frank Hugh O'Donnell together with Sean Murray, Mick Price, Sean MacBride, Roddy Connolly and Peadar O'Donnell. With hindsight, it is difficult to avoid the symbolic conclusion that those five veterans of the struggles of the 1930s were laying more than just an old comrade to rest on that cold, wet winter's morning.[104]

5

'Somewhere out the road in history'
1940–1986

The world into which the young Peadar Joe was brought was materially comfortable and socially and culturally vibrant. The O'Donnell home on Upper Drumcondra Road on the north side of Dublin was a combination of rural Irish visiting house, literary/cultural/political salon, revolutionary safe house, and warm family space. Lile was an art lover and collector, and original paintings and drawings by the likes of Jack B. Yeats and Sean O'Sullivan adorned the walls. Lile's sisters, Geraldine and Jo, lived nearby and spent much time there, as did Peadar's nieces and a daily round of visitors from home and abroad. The house was on the itinerary of literary and left-wing visitors to Dublin, including J.T. Farrell, the socialist Irish-American writer and critic, who called in July 1938. An admirer of *Islanders* who was excited about meeting this 'old IRA fighter', he was shocked to discover that O'Donnell was 'a Stalinist' who dismissed Farrell's pessimistic talk of the inevitability of war. They shared tea, which along with coffee was Peadar's tipple of choice. He never smoked tobacco or drank alcohol. 'I am one of those freak Irishmen', as he put it, 'who deny themselves the comfort of the public house; deny is not the word, it is just a world off my beat.'[1]

The O'Donnells were financially well off, due primarily to Lile's inherited wealth. Peadar's royalties provided a further income, while they had built up a substantial shareholding in Pye Radio, which dominated the expanding Irish radio market in the 1930s and 1940s. He explained his involvement in shares by saying it was 'playing the capitalists at their own game. If you play rugby, you don't go by the rules of soccer', a similar explanation to that given by that other shareholder,

Karl Marx. Besides art, visits to the dog track and foreign trips, fast cars were his main indulgence. O'Donnell was generous with his money, helping his nieces through school and nursing college; sponsoring students at the Workers' College; meeting campaign debts and offering a helping hand to penniless writers and others in need. Honor Tracy, who worked with him when he edited *The Bell* magazine, likened him to a 'benevolent patriarch' who with 'feudal generosity . . . spread his wing over all who were friendless or in need'. He had a huge network of contacts in the upper echelons of the state, business and the media, but utilized them primarily for the benefit of others or the pursuit of 'the common good', an extension of the aristocratic benevolence identified by Tracy.[2]

Peadar O'Donnell had been at the centre of Irish revolutionary politics for over two decades. He had relished the activism, and his optimism and belief in the potential of republicanism to deliver revolutionary change – sustained by the support of his allies on the republican left and in the Irish and international communist movement – gave him the energy to persevere against the odds throughout the 1920s and 1930s. But by 1940, the decidedly non-revolutionary Fianna Fáil had established hegemony not only over republicanism, but over the majority of the Irish working class; the IRA was reduced to a militarist, apolitical rump; socialist republicanism had seen its hopes perish with Republican Congress; the CPI was a tiny, ineffective force on its last legs; Franco was triumphant in Spain while Nazi Germany was in the ascendant in Europe and allied to the Soviet Union. O'Donnell was now entering his late forties and had just acquired parental responsibilities, encouraging him, in the words of his adopted son, to 'pull in his horns'. His energy was undiluted, but he now began to direct it in a different way. He reconciled himself with the 'state machine' he had until recently pledged to destroy, to the extent of becoming one of its cogs, albeit a minor one. He also established, managed and later edited a liberal journal that was a vehicle for cultural opposition and radical exposure rather than socialist analysis and class politics. Here, then, at the midway point of his long life, Peadar O'Donnell began a period of (relatively) 'peaceful co-existence' with the state and the system that would last until his death.

The Emergency

On the outbreak of the Second World War in September 1939, de Valera declared Ireland's neutrality. Besides an obvious desire to avoid the horrors of war, it was the policy that was least divisive politically and was symbolically important in allowing the state to demonstrate its sovereignty and independence. A major danger to de Valera's careful wartime policy was the IRA, which under the leadership of Russell had declared 'war' on Britain and launched a bombing campaign there in January 1939. This posed a direct threat to de Valera's pledge on the return of the ports in 1938 that Ireland would not be used as a base for attacks on Britain. In June 1939 he had armed himself with the draconian Offences Against the State Act, and under the Emergency Powers Act of September 1939 added to his repressive arsenal. The Emergency offered both an added impetus and an ideal opportunity for the elimination of the IRA from Irish politics. Fianna Fáil achieved it through a combination of internment, military courts, the death penalty and censorship. The Northern Ireland government undertook a similar policy.

Supportive of neutrality and fearful both that the IRA's militarism and absence of politics would pull it into alliance with the Nazis, and that a continuation on its current path would lead to the final destruction of what they regarded as a noble tradition, Peadar O'Donnell and George Gilmore published an appeal to it on the outbreak of war to cease operations and dump arms until the war was over.[3] It fell on deaf ears. In December 1939 two IRA men, James McCormick (aka Frank Richards) and Peter Barnes were sentenced to death in Britain for causing an explosion in Coventry in August that had killed five civilians. The bomb had exploded accidentally and the two men were widely believed to be innocent. The sentencing unleashed a wave of bitterness across Ireland and a strong campaign for reprieve developed, backed by the government. O'Donnell organized a petition signed by a number of Irish writers setting out the innocence of the men and the fact that the explosion had been accidental. In a memo sent to John Maffey, the British diplomatic representative in Ireland, O'Donnell explained that the IRA campaign was aimed at securing headlines in the world press to highlight the 'conspiracy of silence on the partition of Ireland' and was the work of 'confused idealists'. The men were hanged in February 1940.[4]

In the meantime, IRA activities in Ireland led to the abandonment of any lingering leniency from de Valera. He stood fast in the face of hunger strikes and in April 1940 two strikers died. Anxious to prevent the creation of public sympathy, severe censorship was used to 'kill public interest', leading to even further anger on the part of republicans. O'Donnell addressed a protest meeting in Dublin at which he called for the censorship to be 'burst' through mass demonstrations.[5] At the 1940 annual general meeting of the Academy of Letters, O'Donnell suggested that the body should interest itself in politics, in order to heighten its public profile. His proposal that it should fundraise for the dependants of IRA internees was rejected, though a one-off fundraising event was agreed to.[6] Repression intensified, as elements in the IRA began collaboration with the Nazis, and O'Donnell appears to have backed off in his support, influenced also perhaps by his employment by the state (see below). In any event, the IRA became splintered in the summer of 1941, and by the autumn was no longer a serious threat.

In the summer of 1940 the country was gripped by the fear of invasion following the end of the 'Phoney War' and the fall of France. The government and opposition buried Civil War divisions and shared platforms to promote a national defence and recruitment effort. O'Donnell and Gilmore seized the opportunity to give the old Republican Congress/united front line a final airing in a detailed leaflet entitled 'Invasion!'. The key to rallying the people, they argued, was not inviting Fine Gael onto a defence council while interning republicans, but for Fianna Fáil to make peace with the IRA and 'unite separatists' in support of neutrality. They admitted that the IRA was undergoing 'a very unfortunate period' but believed it could be rescued from its fascistic elements by the organization of a democratic mass movement based on local defence committees. They ended with the slogans: 'No Part in the Fight between Britain and Germany in Ireland', and 'Unity for the Republic and Neutrality'. Needless to say, nothing came of their plan.[7] The government indulged in rhetorical anti-partitionism throughout the war, and put it forward as one of the reasons for neutrality, but ironically its existence (allowing the Allies a crucial foothold on the island) was one of the factors contributing to the survival of the policy. The O'Donnells moved between Dublin and their new house in Meenmore during the war years, and in December 1940 Peadar spoke at an anti-partition rally in Dungloe, where he shared a platform with Fianna Fáil TDs and Derry's Nationalist MP. The rally was part of a campaign for an 'Ulster Convention' as a preliminary to a 'National Convention' on partition. O'Donnell described partition as 'an outrage against the nation' and saw a convention as an opportunity to put it on 'the world stage'.[8]

Despite his record of anti-fascism, it is interesting to note O'Donnell's belief in the primacy of neutrality and Irish 'national' concerns in his attitude to the war. He clearly wished to see the defeat of the Nazis, but refused to accept the bona fides of British imperialists as champions of the anti-fascist struggle. He shared the dominant attitude in Ireland, which was the government's public line backed by its wartime censorship policy, that this was a war between rival imperialist powers in which Ireland needed to do what it could to avoid being a mere 'pawn'.[9] The government operated a secret policy of support for the Allies, and also allowed Irish nationals to join the Allied forces and work in the British war economy, an approach supported by O'Donnell who thought that de Valera's 'double game' policy (public maintenance of strict neutrality, secret support of Allied war effort) was both clever and justified. Neutrality, he wrote after the war, 'expressed the most positive form on which partitioned Ireland could be expected to take a stand'.[10] With the entry of the Soviet Union into the war in June 1941, the CPI altered its policy to one of support for the British war effort and opposition to Irish neutrality. This led to its increased isolation and in July its only surviving southern branch in Dublin was dissolved, leaving the party organized only in Northern Ireland, to where Sean Murray departed to work in the shipyards. He played only a subsidiary role in the party there. O'Donnell later accused the communists of committing a 'crime' in undervaluing and underutilizing a man he regarded as 'the greatest thing we in Ireland produced since Connolly'.[11] Most of the remaining communists joined the Labour Party in Dublin, which at this time was undergoing a rapid grassroots expansion and radicalization. Many workers who had been radicalized by the campaigns against the government's reactionary wartime policies, particularly the Trade Union Bill and Wages Standstill Order, joined up, and there was what one participant called 'a brief but memorable flowering' of left-wing politics in Dublin. The same writer noted that a feature of this radical activity was the absence of the former Republican Congress leaders.[12] O'Donnell, indeed, appears not to have partaken in the many large demonstrations and campaigns (housing, social welfare, etc.) that were a feature of the first years of the Emergency.

On the outbreak of war, the British launched a recruitment drive for labour in Ireland and tens of thousands of Irish men and women travelled to work in the war economy. In February 1942 Peadar O'Donnell was appointed as the government's Advisor on Migratory Labour, attached to the Department of Industry and Commerce, on a substantial salary of £40 per month. He was based in Dublin Castle, but travelled to Britain frequently, reporting on conditions and advising the Irish authorities on policy. As the war progressed the 'moral danger' posed to the thousands of young Irish women in England moved to the top of the agenda and in early 1944 the Department of External Affairs instructed the Irish High Commissioner in London to investigate the various residential 'camps' where Irish women workers were billeted. O'Donnell was centrally involved in the survey, and his reports throw fascinating light on his apparently unproblematic sharing of the paternalistic, sexist Catholic 'moral policing' approach that dominated Irish church and state attitudes to women. His memo on a visit to Burghfield Residential Camp near Reading in February 1944 reported that 'unfortunately a considerable strength of American forces are camped nearby' and that the girls socialized with them in pubs and at dances. He criticized the 'passivity' of the camp's welfare officer and her Irish assistant, and reported his suggestion to them that they should acquire the services of an Irishwoman who worked at a nearby hostel,

> who by the simple expedient of saying the rosary in the Chapel Hut nightly, organised a collective Big Sister and had a very good influence on the few wild ones. I argued that this was really but another form of woman police which the circumstances had compelled in many parts of Britain.[13]

The flow of emigrants slowed to a trickle as travel and security restrictions were imposed by the British government in the run-up to the Normandy landings, and in June 1944 O'Donnell's post was terminated.

The Bell

Peadar O'Donnell's other 'job' during the war was as managing editor of *The Bell*, a new monthly magazine he founded in 1940. The idea of a broadranging cultural magazine had been with him since his prison days, and now, with the war restricting the availability of British journals and magazines, and limiting the outlets for Irish writing and writers, O'Donnell resurrected the concept and set about making it a reality. He approached Joseph McGrath, a former TD and now a successful businessman with a taste for cultural patronage, who gave him £1,000. He then secured the services of Ireland's pre-eminent 'man of letters', Sean O'Faolain, as editor, a crucial factor in giving the new venture the 'stature' that O'Donnell wanted for it. He joined O'Faolain on the editorial board and they launched *The Bell* in October 1940.[14] In his opening editorial O'Faolain set out their vision. *The Bell* would be not only a literary review, but also a magazine of life as it was lived in Ireland at that time. It did not have a 'policy' but a 'character' that would be formed by the contributors and readers. The aim was to celebrate the plurality and diversity of social and cultural life, and challenge the idealized abstractions of 'official' culture.[15] It was pioneering in its reflective, reflexive and critical agenda, and in its combination of investigative and analytical features with high quality fiction and essays from new and established writers. As well as managing its affairs, O'Donnell contributed eleven times to *The Bell* during O'Faolain's tenure, which lasted until March 1946: eight socio-political and cultural pieces, two (short) short stories, and a draft first chapter of the novel that had been rudely interrupted by civil wars in Achill and Spain, eventually published as *The Big Windows* in 1955.

His non-fiction contributions almost all touched on the twin themes that would dominate his editorial concerns in the post-war period: emigration and the role of the writer in society – 'If only Frank O'Connor had a job in a pawn shop!'[16] Interestingly, besides some passing references, O'Donnell did not participate in the campaign of exposure and criticism of Irish literary censorship that became a feature of the magazine, and which was a factor in forcing the establishment of an appeals mechanism at the war's end. One possible contributory factor for its lack of priority for him was that, almost alone of his generation of writers, none of his books was banned. O'Faolain's conscientious editorship helped and encouraged a generation of new writers, and both he and O'Donnell were instrumental in launching the career of the young Brendan Behan during this period. The nineteen-year-old was imprisoned for IRA activities from 1942 to 1946, and it was O'Donnell who championed his cause in the war years and led the campaign to persuade the authorities to allow publication of his writings, telling the Department of Justice that he and O'Faolain regarded Behan as the country's 'most promising writer'. O'Faolain was allowed to see his work and advise the young writer, but the prohibition on publication remained in place until Behan's release in 1946. O'Donnell's relationship with Behan later soured after the latter allegedly drunkenly abused him at a republican gathering, with the result that, as editor of *The Bell* in the early 1950s he apparently refused to publish anything by the man whose career he had helped to start.[17] Another acclaimed writer who gained from O'Donnell's support was Patrick Kavanagh, whom he called 'the man of greatest genius among us'.[18] He published much work of Kavanagh's during his reign as editor, including a serialization of *Tarry Flynn*, which O'Donnell believed was a prime target for the censors, 'but I knew that Jack Piggot and Christy

O'Reilly [of the Censorship Board] would never dare ban a thing I was responsible for'.[19]

By late 1945 O'Faolain was disillusioned and weary. He edited his last issue in March 1946 and was replaced by O'Donnell, who continued as editor until he wound up *The Bell* in 1954. The writer James Plunkett described the magazine's change of personality well:

> O'Faolain's *Bell* reflected his own sharp sightedness and polemical skill. With the height of good manners it could poleaxe an opponent and its characteristics were courage (rare in those days) and intellectual muscle. Peadar's had another kind of strength – physical muscle perhaps, if that will serve at all adequately to describe his habit of testing theory against life to encourage his writers to dig more deeply into the thought patterns of people in their ordinary environment for aspects of that elusive article – Irish Reality.[20]

'His writers', much to his dismay, failed to pursue his agenda. O'Donnell's idea was that writers alone were in a position to give voice and coherence to the dissatisfaction that existed in post-war Ireland, with its 'crumbling population' and pervasive 'feeling of frustration and defeat and distrust'. They alone could 'startle people out of their sense of personal failure into a realization that they are, in fact, victims of criminal neglect'. His own generation of writers (O'Faolain, O'Connor, O'Flaherty, O'Casey) had emerged from the revolutionary period and the republican tradition. When the generation of Yeats and AE 'peeled off with the Treaty', those new writers 'tore at the romantic Ireland' presented by their predecessors, before raging against the 'yahooism' of the new rulers, who struck back at them with censorship.[21] The new generation was faced with a less clear-cut task, and O'Donnell presented them with a challenge and urged them to take it up. He identified the isolation of writers from the community that had developed during the war as a key problem and believed that the lack of a cadre of independent, professional writers 'which is necessary for a wholesome public spirit' was a major block.[22] He urged writers to organize, reject individualism and counter the isolation that only led to defeatism and pessimism, by reconnecting with their community.

With regard to cultural policy, O'Donnell characteristically focused on the positive rather than the negative. While acknowledging the continuing blight of censorship, he argued for positive measures such as the development of an Irish publishing industry and the establishment of a Ministry of Arts. He believed that the campaign against censorship lacked the sense of gaiety that should mark movements for progressive change, and suggested an annual ceremonial waking, replete with 'keeners', of that year's most important banned books.[23] He rejected the view being propagated in foreign journals that censorship was clerically driven and blamed lay religious zealots who forced priests 'to do their bidding'. (Likewise, and betraying a cynicism about the Irish 'masses' at odds with his pre-war views, he challenged the 'myth' of reactionary trade union leaders holding back a socialist rank and file, and argued that, North and South, they had been 'forced into reactionary roles by their members'.)[24] He developed this point in an article in February 1954, which was a response to Paul Blanchard's *The Irish and Catholic Power*. Rejecting the 'false notion' that a definite form of social behaviour was associated with Catholicism, he wrote: 'Protestant and Catholic zealots in conflict have a common political aim, to keep the country politically divided . . . the Catholic Hierarchy and the Grand Lodge of the Orange Order are objectively on the same side on social and political issues. *In a setting of such confusion the problem is not how to achieve great revolutionary change, but first steps of a progressive character.*'[25] [Emphasis mine].

That last comment encapsulated O'Donnell's transformation from revolutionary to reformist, which was in line with that of his communist comrades. He generally wrote within the parameters of post-war communist policy. In March 1951, for example, he responded to an article in which O'Faolain criticized 'anti-Americanism'. O'Donnell rejected his friend's praise of the effects of Marshall Aid in Italy and presented it as part of the capitalist Pax Americana, a bulwark against communism. Ireland, he wrote, should 'remedy underdevelopment and stand for peace, or failing peace, neutrality, [rather] than . . . seek alms and surrender to war plans on which we can have no influence'.[26] This was precisely in tune with the communist line in the cold war era. Following the death of Stalin in March 1953, there was a shift in policy again, and the communists became committed to 'peaceful co-existence' between east and west. O'Donnell was active in the communist Peace Campaign Committee, and was a delegate to the World Peace Conference in Budapest in June 1953 where the idea of 'peaceful co-existence' was put forward, and it was echoed by him in the pages of *The Bell*. In his final article in November 1954, in what turned out to be the penultimate issue, he promoted the idea of east-west trade, a key component of peaceful co-existence, as a solution to the problems of the west and Irish economic underdevelopment. He himself had acted as a one-man trade delegation in arranging the export of Donegal herring to Czechoslovakia, and he encouraged the Irish government to establish diplomatic and trade relations with the Eastern Bloc countries. In another contribution to the new era, he organized a cultural visit by a group of Irish writers to the Soviet Union in January 1955.

The writer he asked to lead the delegation was Anthony Cronin, who had acted as his associate editor on *The Bell* in its final years. Cronin, regarded by O'Donnell a promising young writer who might spearhead his campaign to shake up the new generation, was in fact more representative of the cynicism and individualism that O'Donnell wanted challenged. He was part of the alcohol-centred bohemianism of 1950s Dublin, a world that was alien to O'Donnell. In his autobiographical novel *The Life of Riley*, Cronin gives a wicked and hilarious caricature of the persona of the mid-century Peadar O'Donnell. He appears in the book as Prunchios McGonaghy – 'patriotic man of letters' with friends in high places, editor of *The Trumpet* and author of 'tweedy Marxist novels about peasants and fishermen' – who socialized with parish priests and 'regime intellectuals' and encouraged Riley to live in the slums in order to get a finger on the pulse of the people, and an understanding of the dialectic.[27]

Cronin's frustrations with *The Bell* and O'Donnell's editorship, evident in both the novel and the memoir, *Dead as Doornails*, are echoed, albeit within a context of fondness, in the accounts of others who worked on the magazine at the time. Among others, Val Mulkerns recalls 'an editor who hated editing'.[28] He kept *The Bell* afloat in the face of burgeoning costs and falling circulation with ingenious fundraising schemes such as organizing the installation of litter bins on lamp-posts across Dublin, funded by the advertisements they carried, with the surplus (revenue, not rubbish!) going to the magazine. In April 1948 it was forced to suspend publication when O'Donnell's plan to go fundraising in the US was scuppered by the refusal of the American authorities to grant him a visa because he 'held certain beliefs', which were unwelcome in the McCarthyite red scare days of the cold war. He learned that someone had passed on a copy of Hogan's *Could Ireland Become Communist?* to an official, and this had sealed his fate.[29] *The Bell* returned in November 1950, but was reduced to a quarterly from the summer of 1953 until its demise in December 1954.

O'Faolain was occasionally embarrassed in later years by the common assumption that he had created *The Bell*, and in 1970 wrote to the *Irish Times* to clarify that it was, 'from start to finish, Peadar O'Donnell's creation . . . he kept it going, for fourteen years in all . . . a remarkable feat for what may be called, in his name, a one-man Little Magazine.' Giving the impression of two people shoving a slightly poisoned chalice back and forth, O'Donnell leapt into print to declare '*The Bell*, as the public knew it, was Sean O'Faolain's creation.' He went on to repeat his frequent assertion that he should have ended it with O'Faolain – 'I even thought it at the time.'[30] *The Bell* had played an important role in wartime Ireland, but O'Donnell's failure to make it relevant afterwards may have been the result of larger forces than his own failings. Richard Kearney, for example, has argued that post-war Ireland had become partitionist not only in the geographical sense, but also in 'an intellectual sense, based on the premise that the socio-political debate dealing with reality and the literary debate dealing with imaginative vision, should be kept rigidly apart.'[31]

Post-*Bell*(um)

Besides *The Bell*, much of O'Donnell's time between 1948 and 1954 was taken up with work related to his membership of a governmental Commission on Emigration and other Population Problems. The Commission was established by the new inter-party government in April 1948.[32] Its brief was to 'investigate the causes and consequences of the present level and trend in population' and to make recommendations for a 'national population policy'. Although it was hoped at the outset to have a report by 1949, it was not completed until mid-1954. The principal reason for the delay was the need for updated statistics, requiring the commissioning of a new census in 1951, which showed increased emigration and depopulation and thus led to a further expansion of enquiries. The full Commission met 115 times, and O'Donnell was also involved in various hearings and sub-committees related to the enquiries during that time.

The final 400-page report was packed with details and recommendations. Its overall thrust was that the key to population increase, which it recommended as national policy, was increased and more efficient agricultural productivity.[33] Twelve reservations from commission members were recorded in the report. O'Donnell's reservation was two-fold: firstly, he disagreed with 'the emphasis on subjective factors' in the section on the causes of mass emigration; he saw the cause as essentially economic and thought that the problem could only be remedied by 'the expansion of the whole national economy'. Secondly, he regarded the inclusion of a section on the 'moral and religious deterioration of emigrants' as mistaken, saying that there was no more justification for 'a paragraph on moral delinquency among exiles than in relation to life in Ireland itself.[34] No meaningful action was taken by the government in response to the report.

In 1955 O'Donnell published *The Big Windows*, by common consent his finest literary achievement. The story is centred on islander Brigid Dugan, who arrives with her new husband Tom into his mother Mary's house in a cloistered Donegal glen at the beginning of the twentieth century. Along with Brigid, we learn about the strange and ancient customs, traditions and codes that have survived in this isolated place. Brigid symbolizes progress and change, which is, like her, initially feared and resisted, but eventually, like her, embraced and accepted. The darkness of the glen is a metaphor for its backwardness, and the light, which pours into the house when Brigid has her wish and big windows are installed, symbolizes progress. She befriends an ostracized 'mad woman', brings the first doctor to the glen and becomes a peacemaker due to her refusal to be imprisoned by old disagreements and prejudices. When she departs at the end, following the death of her husband, the glen she leaves behind is a changed place, but changed, we are invited to believe, for the better. The wealth of detail is astonishing, and O'Donnell manages to record and convey a way of life that had gone forever. His flowing prose style is a new departure; stylistically, this is his most complex and assured novel, reflecting a writer at the height of his powers, but also perhaps the more relaxed context and longer time in which it was written. The reviews at the time, and on its reissue in 1983, were universally positive. Benedict Kiely described it as O'Donnell's 'masterpiece . . . a superb work of art'. Sean Breslin called it a landmark in Irish literature: 'With this book, it is possible to argue, O'Donnell does for the novel what Synge did for drama; he expresses a life that had not yet found expression.' For Alan Pryce-Jones, editor of the *Times Literary Supplement*, it was amongst the best novels of the twentieth century.[35]

Throughout the 1950s, with emigration spiralling out of control, O'Donnell, in articles, letters to the press and at public meetings, pointed out that seasonal migration was being replaced by permanent emigration (as he predicted during the war) and that houses were now being 'closed down'. This he saw as the most disturbing development: it was no longer just that the young 'overflow' was leaving, but the very homes that produced the youth of the west were disappearing. He continued to pursue his individual campaign on behalf of emigrants, and in 1956 caused some diplomatic embarrassment when he visited the Irish Centre in London and described it as a 'doss-house'.[36]

Unemployment was the other scourge of the 1950s, and a new unemployed workers' movement emerged in Dublin in 1953–4, with a strong communist involvement. In early 1957 an Unemployed Protest Committee (UPC) was formed, and when an election was called for April, the UPC decided to run a candidate in Dublin. With anti-communism alive again following the Soviet invasion of Hungary in 1956, building worker and former republican internee, Jack Murphy, was chosen over the communist Sam Nolan. Peadar O'Donnell was a 'moving spirit' of the campaign, securing the £100 deposit and contributions to campaign funds from his business contacts, whose willingness to help highlighted the non-socialist nature of the campaign, which presented unemployment as 'a national disgrace' and later (fatally) sought the support of the arch-reactionary Archbishop McQuaid of Dublin. Murphy won the seat, while Fianna Fáil won the election and brought in a severe budget, including the removal of food subsidies. Murphy and two others began a hunger strike and the UPC sought a meeting with McQuaid in an effort to gain his support. McQuaid met with Murphy alone and began to pressurize him into breaking with the committee on the basis that the communists were using him. In August he broke with the UPC and eventually in July 1958, yielding to the personal pressure of McQuaid and political pressure in the media and the Dáil, resigned his seat (which was won by Fianna Fáil), and emigrated to Canada. The whole debâcle destroyed the UPC and was a major setback for the unemployed movement.[37]

The grand (angry) old man

Peadar O'Donnell was in his late sixties as Ireland entered the 1960s, but he had no intention of retiring gracefully from public or political life. Despite periods of ill health, he remained engaged, though the former activist dynamo was now more the supporter, encourager, adviser and sponsor, as well as symbol and inspiration. His age and stature, together with his gradual abandonment of revolutionary politics in favour of campaigns and 'first steps of a progressive nature' helped to establish him as the grand old man of the Irish left and something of a patron saint of progressive causes. While he gave his time and name to international causes, it was the 'dispersal' of the 'small farm countryside' that particularly motivated him. In February 1968 he wrote: 'Groucho Marx described himself the other day as the last of the angry old men; he is 72. If he is after a world championship I think I should contest his claim. I am older and, maybe, even angrier.'[38]

The Irish Campaign for Nuclear Disarmament (ICND) began in early 1959 and O'Donnell was a member from the beginning; he spoke at the campaign's launch meeting in December 1958 and at many subsequent gatherings. He became ICND president in 1960 and promoted its message throughout the 1960s. The campaign faltered in the 1970s, but O'Donnell remained with it and was an inspirational figure to a new generation of peace activists who revived ICND in 1979.[39] He was also a sponsor of the developing Irish Anti-Apartheid Movement, and spoke at some of its demonstrations and public meetings.[40] In 1966 the same cross-generational liberal-left milieu that produced the latter two movements also gave rise to an Irish campaign against the US war against Vietnam. O'Donnell chaired the first public meeting on the issue in July 1966. The movement against the war developed in 1967, spearheaded by the Quaker-backed Irish Peace Movement, the Union of Students in Ireland and O'Donnell's Irish Voice on Vietnam (IVV), which campaigned for the Irish government to support UN general secretary U Thant's January 1967 call for an end to the bombing of North Vietnam and US withdrawal. The IVV staged a 1,000-strong march to the US embassy in October 1967 and organized a petition in support of an end to the bombing without preconditions. Under O'Donnell's continued chairmanship, it organized another march on the US embassy in November 1969. The thrust of the campaign, and O'Donnell's speeches, was humanitarian and peace-centred, and support was sought on the basis of defending 'a small nation' against 'a powerful nation', and not on the basis of socialist anti-imperialism.[41]

The Irish economy, in the meantime, was undergoing a transformation. Under new Taoiseach, Sean Lemass, who replaced de Valera in 1959, the government sought to arrest chronic emigration and population decline. The small-farming sector, still the main plank of the society and economy of the west, had been the main victim, but the reorientation of development policy in the 1960s served to hasten rather than halt its decline. In the resistance that developed, Peadar O'Donnell saw the potential for the local development movement that he had been advocating since the late 1930s, and hoped that a revival of agrarian struggle would make the small-farm countryside 'the point of rally' yet again. His account of the land annuities campaign, *There Will Be Another Day*, was published in 1963 and inspired a new generation of activists. Government development policy was based on the promotion of economic expansion through industrialization, concentrated on growth centres and capitalized by private investment, particularly foreign investment. The resultant 'rising tide' would then supposedly 'lift all boats', but many saw this policy as a recipe for the further marginalization and decline of peripheral areas of the west. Two key opponents were the activist priest Fr James McDyer of Glencolumbcille, County Donegal and General Michael Costello, director of the Irish Sugar Company, who, together with Peadar O'Donnell, envisaged a radically different solution.

Costello believed that agriculture in the west could be made viable through intensive horticulture and the establishment of co-operative vegetable and fish processing industries; he established Erin Foods as a subsidiary of the Sugar Company in 1959 with the idea of processing and marketing vegetables grown in western co-operatives. McDyer established the Errigal Co-operative Society and with the help of Peadar O'Donnell, who organized the initial subscriptions through the Donegal Association in Dublin, raised enough money to establish a plant for processing co-op grown vegetables in 1962. McDyer sought to extend the experiment by starting a communal farming co-operative but the Land Commission and Departments of Agriculture and Finance opposed the plan. In order to give it political muscle, a series of meetings was held across the west addressed by McDyer, Costello, and O'Donnell among others, where the 'Glencolumbkille miracle', as O'Donnell called it, was put forward as a blueprint for regeneration. This developed into a 'Save the West' campaign, which highlighted areas that were particularly neglected and pressed the government to establish pilot schemes that would be, in O'Donnell's words, 'bridgeheads of hope': for him, this would not only benefit the areas, but be 'launch pads for agitation'. The government eventually established twelve pilot schemes, but they never moved beyond the pilot stage, were too scattered to be effective and made little impact on the surrounding countryside.[42]

The 'Save the West' committees became dominated by local priests, professionals and shopkeepers who concentrated on lobbying and utilizing the clientelist structure of Irish politics, thus becoming, in O'Donnell's words, 'a screen rather than a challenge to government neglect'. He advocated grassroots organization and agitation to win 'a radical, comprehensive State plan for the West'. He rejected the idea that 'local initiative and community development' alone was the cure; this had to be linked to a political campaign for a 'national' solution.[43] That campaign needed to be based on an alliance between small farmers and industrial workers. The Dóchas Co-operative Society emerged in 1965 to provide that link, and O'Donnell was its 'driving force'. It combined a practical loan fund scheme, whereby urban workers were encouraged to support rural co-operative initiatives, with a political stress on the need for joint action against dispersal in the west. In a pamphlet called *The Role of Industrial Workers in the Problems of the West* and in the Dóchas journal *Challenge*, O'Donnell identified the dispersal of western communities as the 'point of sharpest attack' by the new 'establishment' of economists, senior civil servants, bankers and industrialists, and was therefore also 'the point of rally' not only for the west itself, but also for the republican and labour movements.[44]

The non-emergence of a national movement with a political programme and a coherent development plan, allowed the government to deal separately with the different areas, diffusing demands with selective concessions while resisting pressure for structural reform. Costello resigned from Irish Sugar in 1966 and was replaced by thirty-year-old Tony O'Reilly, fresh from his success in transforming Bord Bainne, the state's milk marketing board. O'Reilly was given the task of cutting back the Erin Foods operation to stop it from competing with private enterprise, thus dooming the Errigal Co-op processing enterprise. He declared bluntly: 'You just can't grow vegetables competitively on the hillsides of Donegal.'[45] He rapidly arranged a merger of Erin with the multinational Heinz, so that Erin now supplied Heinz with vegetables that were processed in Britain. The deal marked the beginning of O'Reilly's global capitalist career. In May 1969 he became managing director of Heinz in Britain; by 1973 he was president of Heinz worldwide, going on to become a powerful international media tycoon and major corporate player. Ironically, O'Reilly had a close personal relationship with Peadar O'Donnell, having been a school- and rugby-playing friend of Peadar Joe's. He has described O'Donnell as 'almost *in loco parentis* to me in the summers of the late 1940s', which he spent in the O'Donnell house in Meenmore, while he passed many of his school-year afternoons in the house in Drumcondra Road – where 'Peadar was Uncle Peadar to me and his wife was Auntie Lile'. They maintained their friendship; O'Donnell established contacts for O'Reilly in Eastern Europe during his milk marketing days, and the then global capitalist was among O'Donnell's visitors during his final illness.[46]

Small-farmer agitation, meanwhile, came to be expressed through the 'Land Leagues' that developed around the country in the late 1960s in reaction to the 'cheque book tycoons' who were buying up land. The leagues wanted the Land Commission to acquire large estates and divide them up between local smallholders. A group that emerged in

Westmeath, where there were many such estates, approached O'Donnell for help. He encouraged them to organize, and with the help of
Donal Donnelly and others in Dóchas, a National Land League was
launched in September 1969, with Dan McCarthy, later of the Irish
Creamery Milk Suppliers' Association, as president and O'Donnell as
honorary life president. O'Donnell was its 'agitational adviser' and
guiding spirit as the League scored numerous local successes in having
estates divided up, had representatives elected to county councils,
gained the support of trade unionists like Michael Mullen of the
ITGWU, and ran a well produced paper, *The Countryman*, for two years.
Ultimately, however, Irish entry to the EEC saw national structural
policies displaced by the Common Agricultural Policy, and the small-
holder position disappeared from the policy agenda as the larger
farmers in the Irish Farmers' Association became the voice of rural
Ireland, riding on the wave of initial prosperity.[47]

O'Donnell lent his weight to the anti-EEC campaign that developed in
1970–2, and was a patron of the Common Market Defence Campaign,
which argued against entry on the basis of the threat to the Irish
economy, sovereignty and neutrality. He was delighted by the declaration of the Irish Congress of Trade Unions against EEC entry, but
regarded its leadership's failure to lead a real campaign as a repeat of the
labour movement's opt-out from the independence struggle after 1916.
The Labour Party (along with the CPI, re-formed in 1970, both wings of
Sinn Féin and a range of non-party figures) also opposed entry. Labour
had moved to the left in the 1960s, on the back of increased militancy on
the part of the expanding industrial working class and the influx of intellectuals like Conor Cruise O'Brien. O'Donnell and George Gilmore
publicly endorsed O'Brien in the 1969 election, urging support for him
on the basis of his record in anti-apartheid and anti-Vietnam war activities. As Labour spokesman on Northern Ireland, he had taken part in
and supported the civil rights movement that had arisen there in the late
1960s. However, in 1971 he emerged as a strong critic of the Provisional
IRA and opposed the idea that republican prisoners had political status.
Gilmore denounced and disowned him, but O'Brien was pleasantly
surprised that O'Donnell remained friendly. 'Your fellow Republican
bishop', O'Brien told him, 'has excommunicated me.' O'Donnell
laughed; 'That's the way we bishops are. Some of us excommunicate the
sinner, others just pray for him like I'm praying for you.'[48]

O'Donnell and Gilmore, as representatives of the socialist republican
tradition, had provided inspiration and advice to the new leadership of

the republican movement in the 1960s. The process of rethinking republican strategy followed the disastrous 'border campaign' of 1956–62, and drew on the O'Donnellite notion of the late 1920s/early 1930s of moving beyond militarism and involving the movement in social and economic struggles, with the ultimate aim of a socialist republic. The republican movement split in 1969–70 following the outbreak of the 'Troubles' in Northern Ireland, with the Provisionals representing the resurgence of the Catholic-nationalist militarist tradition, and the Officials attempting to become the vanguard of a broader-based struggle. O'Donnell believed that neither group offered the way forward, and that the only way out of 'the mess we are in' was 'a progressively mass movement with a clearly identifiable working class core in its leadership'. The first step was for the 'undoubtedly dedicated and courageous Republican Movement' to realize that it was not in a position to give that lead, and to make way for such a leadership, emerging from the labour movement, North and South. Referring to the 'mistakes of the early Thirties', he appeared to believe that both wings of republicanism would ultimately pave the way for an updated equivalent of 1930s Fianna Fáil, at best, which would end up serving the interests of the 'tycoons', native and international, at the expense of the working class, small farmers and 'exploited lower middle class'.[49]

As it turned out, no 'progressively mass movement' emerged. The Officials went on to become the Workers' Party, which aspired to winning state power North and South, and briefly challenged the CPI for the leadership of Irish communism before both parties were seriously weakened by the collapse of the Soviet Union. The parliamentary wing of the Workers' Party in the South eventually merged with the reformist Labour Party and the Provisionals – following an armed campaign of over twenty-five years, accompanied by a rhetorical adherence to the aim of a 'socialist republic' – eventually embraced a partitionist, reformist settlement. By the close of the twentieth century, socialist republican ideals remained extant only in a handful of minuscule groups, remnants, it appeared, of Irish history.

The momentous events in Northern Ireland were overshadowed for O'Donnell by the death of Lile in October 1969. He was devastated by the loss and a couple of years later sold the house on Drumcondra Road. He then lived, for various stretches, in a bedsit in Dublin, in the home of Ned Gilligan of the National Land League in Mullingar, and with Peadar Joe and his family, before eventually settling in the home of his old friend Nora Harkin in Monkstown, County Dublin, where he found happiness and contentment for his final seven years. In the early 1970s, he worked on a new novel which would reflect the fate of his beloved Donegal islands in the face of the new 'cash nexus' economy. *Proud Island* was published in 1975 to mixed reviews, most of which acknowledged its power and relevance as a 'parable' and 'allegory' rather than a piece of literature. Gonzalez describes it well as 'a skeletal version of the best of O'Donnell's preceding novels'.[50] It is the story of the slow death of an island, based on Inniskeeragh, the island on which *Islanders* was set, which was finally abandoned in 1955. The herring shoals change their routes and are put out of reach of the islanders' small boats due to a ring of foreign trawlers. The central character, politically conscious Hughie Duffy, knows that larger and better boats are the answer, but the government offers the dole. Land is bought up by outsiders and 'No Trespassing' signs signal the beginning of the end of the community. Emigration and 'dead houses' become the inevitable result.

In the 1980s, O'Donnell began to receive the type of recognition and honour usually bestowed posthumously in Ireland. In November 1982 he was presented with a cheque for $10,000 at a reception in the Abbey, a joint award from the Irish American Cultural Institute, the Irish Institute of New York, and the Ireland Fund – the latter represented by Tony O'Reilly, who surprised many present when he revealed his connection to 'Uncle Peadar'. In June 1984, a Committee of Concerned University Staff at University College Galway, protesting at the conferring of an honorary doctorate on US president Ronald Reagan, staged a 'deconferring ceremony' at which three previous honorary doctorate recipients handed their degrees back to 'Acting Chancellor', Peadar O'Donnell. In January 1985, the same group hosted a 'Tribute to Peadar O'Donnell' at which a composition written in his honour was performed by the group Moving Hearts and O'Donnell spoke about his life in politics. His speech was published the following year as *Monkeys in the Superstructure: Reminiscences of Peadar O'Donnell*. In August 1985, the annual Patrick MacGill Summer School in Donegal was devoted to O'Donnell's life and work. He said he felt like he was attending his own wake. Academics, writers and politicians gathered to assess his politics and literature, and in general to pay tribute, with the exception of Jim Kemmy of the Democratic Socialist Party, who launched a personalized attack on the man he called 'the great bamboozler of the Irish left', because of his links with communism and republicanism and failure to leave behind an organizational or theoretical legacy.[51]

The CPI, the party that he said in 1979 he would join 'if I was a young man today', hosted O'Donnell's final political public engagements. The final piece he wrote for publication was a CPI-produced pamphlet, *Not Yet Emmet* (1985), his account of the Treaty split and his reflections on how 'a great struggle came to so unworthy an end'. It was subtitled *A Wreath on the Grave of Sean Murray*, in honour of his great friend and influence. On 13 May 1986 Peadar O'Donnell died at the age of ninety-three. He left instructions that there were to be 'no priests, no politicians and no pomp' at his funeral, and his wishes were granted. Following cremation at Glasnevin, his ashes were placed on his beloved Lile's family plot in Kilconduff cemetery outside Swinford, County Mayo. 'It is more important how you performed on stage', he used to say to his friend Donal Donnelly, 'than how you exit'.[52]

Conclusion

Revolutionaries shape revolutions, but the converse also applies, and it was Peadar O'Donnell's fate to be more shaped than shaper. As a trade unionist, he was at the centre of a major wave of working-class militancy that failed to move outside labourist parameters and which, when it was politically channelled, flowed into the integrationist tide of bourgeois Irish nationalism. He saw the Treaty as a mere stage in the revolutionary process, and when the labour movement failed to 'push past' it, he invested his hopes, in the absence of an alternative, in a republican movement that proved itself an inappropriate vehicle for social revolution. The pan-class, integrationist and conservative centre of gravity in Irish nationalism proved more powerful than the class-struggling, radical thread that O'Donnell identified with and tried to harness, just as the apolitical, militarist pull of the IRA ultimately prevailed over his 'Citizen Army' vision. The limits of the possible, in socialist terms, continued to be set for O'Donnell by the Stalinist communist movement and the lure of the elusive 'Republic'; the former carried him into the culs-de-sac demanded by Soviet priorities, while the latter became the shrink-wrapped property of Fianna Fáil, before being attached as a term to the twenty-six-county state by the first interparty government. The opportunity to mount a final challenge to Fianna Fáil hegemony arose with Republican Congress, but for a variety of reasons, O'Donnell et al. chose to attack the dominant party, as Dunphy has pointed out,[1] not at its weakest point (class) but at its strongest (nation): there could only be one winner at that stage. He subsequently came to accept, de facto, the southern state, and his agenda moved from the revolutionary to the radical reformist. His retreat from revolution was eased (some critics have argued, propelled)[2] by his materially comfortable position, as well as his reserves of 'cultural capital', which allowed him to assume the 'safe' role of cultural dissident and patron. He remained, however, a radical voice and principled dissident, and his history and enduring stature made him a living icon for new generations of radicals.

Although he retained the belief that the republican movement continued to represent 'the highest concentrate of selfless, courageous dedication to national service in the country',[3] O'Donnell disappointed many in both wings of that revived movement following the outbreak of the Troubles by remaining true to his further belief that it could not provide the solution to the Northern question. In August 1931 he wrote that nationalists and republicans in the North had to fall in behind and encourage a radical working-class movement, it being the only formation that could lead the attack against imperialism;[4] he repeated this again in the 1970s. In the meantime the Republican Congress had tried and failed to create such a movement. Congress broke new ground in grappling with the issue of unionist resistance, and in its (ultimately symbolic) successes in bringing working-class Protestants under a republican banner. In the 1980s, O'Donnell linked his hopes for change in the North to developments in Britain, where the disappearance of the monarchy in the face of 'the socialism' of the British working class was the key to breaking the reactionary hold of unionism over the Northern Irish Protestant working class.[5] With his beloved 'small-farm countryside' becoming another remnant of history and an even less likely 'point of rally' than in the past, his hopes for progress in the South became vested in trade unions and new social movements: 'everywhere progressive things are being fought', he told a young audience in 1985, 'rally to it. It's out of the sum total of these progressive things that we'll produce something in the end.'[6]

His stature as 'grand old man of the Irish left', while merited in many ways, also owed much to the lack of competition. The same could not be said in the literary field, where he has only recently begun to gain the recognition his writing deserves. O'Donnell was obviously a gifted novelist, but from the outset his fiction was written with a clear political purpose. He had no interest, he often said, in being viewed as a creative artist alone, and his reputation and stature as a political activist has doubtlessly contributed to the relative critical neglect of his fiction. Another shadow was cast by the achievements of his brilliant contemporaries, O'Connor, O'Faolain and O'Flaherty. Yeats and O'Flaherty, as we have seen, expressed regret that O'Donnell's political activities interfered with the realization of his creative potential. Following the publication of *There Will Be Another Day* (1963), Maurice Kennedy declared him 'the most maddening of Irish writers' who had been 'promising' for almost forty years; he wished he would 'buckle down' and fulfil that promise. It was not to be, and the reading public, as Kennedy ruefully concluded, had to be 'content with what he [gave] us when the spirit move[d] him'.[7] Francis Doherty saw O'Donnell the writer as 'suffering the fate of having too many reputations, having made his mark on too many fields'. Writing in 1990, he argued that, as 'one of Ireland's greatest regional novelists', O'Donnell belatedly and 'richly deserves our attention'. The American academic, Alexander Gonzalez, has likewise argued that, 'taken collectively, O'Donnell's works achieve a regional depth comparable to Hardy's Wessex'. His interest in O'Donnell was aroused when he noticed how little critical attention was given to him, 'the mere mention of his name often serving in place of conscientious literary scrutiny.' He began to examine his literature more closely, a process that culminated in the first book devoted solely to O'Donnell's writing: *Peadar O'Donnell: A Readers' Guide* (1997). Gonzalez concluded that, while his entire canon is of too uneven a quality for him to be rated among the 'first rank' of Irish novelists, much of his writing was of the 'highest order'. Most recently, Terry Eagleton has hailed O'Donnell's 'superb fiction'.[8] Perhaps the greatest tribute, and the one O'Donnell would have appreciated for its capturing of his objectives, came from Sean O'Faolain:

> Peadar is one of the few writers who can visualise freedom through his living characters. Peadar knows that it is a matter of community living and basic human needs in the country or in the city. He gets down to the soil and the roots. Anyone who wants to know what freedom is about should read Peadar O'Donnell.[9]

The subtle politics of O'Donnell's fiction is highlighted when it is compared to the work of two of his other contemporaries and friends, Liam O'Flaherty and Seamus Ó Grianna. As Michael D. Higgins has pointed out, O'Flaherty and O'Donnell use similar materials of Irish island and rural life, but while the resolution of political and economic contradictions is sought by O'Flaherty in terms of individual salvation, in O'Donnell's fiction 'an individual's fate fades into insignificance in comparison with the community's comprehension of what changes are taking place'.[10] Ó Grianna's imaginative world occupied precisely the same corner of Donegal as O'Donnell's, and while there are many similarities between their respective detailed depictions of life there, their approaches are radically different. Ó Grianna's characters, for example, are passive in the face of their impoverished and harsh circumstances, while O'Donnell's generally try to fight back and collectively shape their own destinies. When Ó Grianna deals with the national struggle, it is presented in terms of individual and national heroism, whereas O'Donnell is always careful to identify the social and collective dimension. Both writers portray the neighbourliness that they experienced while growing up, but for O'Donnell it is always the key to survival and, beyond that, if harnessed and properly directed, a force for radical social change.[11]

Another possible reason for the neglect of O'Donnell is the fact that his writing harmonized with the subsequently discredited 'official culture' of post-independence Ireland, with its idealization of the west, valorization of peasant life, and so on. O'Donnell himself rejected the hypocrisy of this culture, and was interested only in the preservation and celebration of living communities: 'I hate to see spinning-wheels, thatched cottages, small farms and handicraft kept alive to make a show.' He railed against the idealization of the western Gaeltachts while emigration and poverty were decimating them, declaring that 'the best step towards a new cultural life is a sharp rise in the standards of living'.[12]

O'Donnell had a clear view of his own role as a writer, but failed to convince many of his fellow artists to fulfil what he saw as their duty. While acknowledging the genius of O'Casey, for example, he was disappointed that he failed to portray a spirit of resistance in his working-class characters, believing that many of his plays merely gave 'the fat Dublin middle class' a chance to laugh at the proletariat. He hated *The Plough and the Stars* because there was no character 'from whom any revolutionary action could proceed'. While not as narrow as many of his fellow republicans in the interwar period in judging all literature in terms of its propaganda value, he was unsympathetic to O'Faolain's and O'Connor's initial concern with publicly burying their 'dead illusions' about the Irish revolution, believing that, until they could offer a 'better way to liberty', those illusions were still 'life giving in a large section of our youth'. By the late 1940s he had come to reassess the role of the post-independence realists, acknowledging their contribution in raging against the 'yahooism' of the new native rulers and the fact that they had at least reflected real life. By then O'Donnell had long since abandoned hopes of fomenting revolutionary change, and campaigned for writers to at least engage with reality and reflect ordinary lives, which he saw as the first step. He believed that 'brave writing will have to wait on brave living' and that in 'crumbling' post-war Ireland any sort of writing that was 'of the people' was all that could be expected.[13]

One of his criticisms of O'Casey was that the women in his plays were 'as patient as donkeys, they accepted their lot without revolt'.[14] A feature of O'Donnell's own female characters is their strength; they are at least as significant and active as men, and often more so. There is little idealization, however, and women are just as likely to be reactionary figures (Mrs Garvey in *On the Edge of the Stream*), as heroic freedom fighters (Nuala Godfrey Dhu in *The Knife*). One of his most interesting characters is Nelly McFadden in *On the Edge of the Stream*, for whom the personal becomes political in O'Donnell's most explicitly feminist novel.

His egalitarian and progressive political views alone are not sufficient to explain his empathy with and admiration for women. He grew up in a strongly matriarchal community, where women bore the burdens while men were absent for half the year. His mother was a strong, progressively thinking woman who obviously influenced him greatly; Lile, his wife, likewise; and, as he said himself, he worked with a 'great generation of women who were both political and social revolutionaries'.[15] He meant a political generation, for his comrades included radical activists from across the age spectrum, such as Charlotte Despard, Hanna Sheehy Skeffington and Cora Hughes. O'Donnell welcomed the growth of the second-wave feminist movement in the 1970s and believed, like Connolly, that 'you can judge how advanced a movement is by its position on women'.[16] His record is strong on gender equality issues. A core issue in his first major strike, at the Monaghan asylum, was his insistence on an equal pay rise for women; he demanded equal dole payments for women in the late 1930s, and made the subservient position accorded to women a plank of his objection to the 1937 constitution. Given all of this, his 'woman police' attitudes during the war are a little jarring, but show the extent to which, while opposing the zealotry of Catholic actionists (whether the hymn-singing mobs of the 1930s, Maria Duce in the 1950s or the proponents of the anti-abortion referendum in the 1980s), he could also share some of the dominant patriarchal attitudes that ran deep in his society .

O'Donnell remained a Catholic all his life (though he appears to have become increasingly non-practising after the death of Lile) and had many friends among the clergy. Rather than being 'anti-clerical', as he was often branded, he was, if anything, 'pro-clerical', friendly with many priests and consistently defending clerics whom he saw as being, more often than not, pushed into reactionary roles by lay zealots and political bishops. Like Connolly, he highlighted those aspects of Christianity that supported his socialist views, with that mixture of sincerity and strategy forced upon the socialist agitator in a highly religious country. O'Donnell opposed the involvement of priests in politics, except when they supported his own position, and did not concur with the correspondent in *An Phoblacht* who suggested that 'the best way to discourage the political priest is to keep him off the political platform, even when he is championing us'.[17] He related his 'enemies, lay and clerical, to the interests they serve[d]',[18] rarely pushing his analysis beyond a crude economic determinism centred on the 'base' and 'superstructure' paradigm. He did not have access to the writings of his contemporary, the Italian Marxist, Antonio Gramsci, which have helped radicals of later generations to see the reactionary hegemonic role of the Catholic Church, for example, or how republicanism could develop autonomously as an ultimately conservative force. He did, however, share with Gramsci a belief in the importance of grassroots organization and subaltern popular struggle, and the idea of the collective intellectual; he was a consistent encourager of what Gramsci called the organic intellectual, while in his most active and revolutionary phase, O'Donnell was the embodiment of Gramsci's philosophy of praxis. His self-admitted reluctance to develop his own theoretical ideas, however, meant that such tendencies were inevitably subsumed by the elitist assumptions intrinsic to both the Leninist and Irish separatist traditions, to which he always deferred. It also led him to exaggerate the significance of narrow thinkers like Sean Murray and Liam Mellows.

Like the communists, O'Donnell welcomed the emergence of progressive individuals and ideas within the Church in the 1960s. Sharing a platform with Fr McDyer during the 'Save the West' campaign, he looked at the priest and said, 'I do not know whether I have moved to the right or the Church has moved to the left!'[19] Perhaps it was a bit of both. O'Donnell always espoused a secular and anti-sectarian republicanism and opposed the idea of a state or 'semi-state' Church. However, it is interesting to note that his first clearly articulated opposition to the incorporation of Catholic social and moral teaching into the law of the land, which had been ongoing since independence, was in relation to de Valera's constitution, and then it was in terms of the barriers it erected to unification and the issue of private property, rather than as being intrinsically problematic in itself. He opposed the philistine and draconian censorship of literature that developed in post-independence Ireland, though not as vociferously as many of his contemporaries. His position on freedom of expression was ambiguous. He participated in the newspaper-burning activities of republicans during the War of Independence and Civil War, and in the 'no free speech for traitors' campaign against Cumann na nGaedheal following Fianna Fáil's accession to power. As editor of *An Phoblacht*, moreover, he facilitated the cultural exclusivist strain of the censorship mentality. Like his uncritical support of neutrality during the Second World War, however, the 'national' dimension always outweighed any commitment to abstract ideals.

He was, of course, one of the few good Irish writers not to be banned, and his comment (with regard to publishing extracts from *Tarry Flynn* in *The Bell*) that the censors 'would never dare ban a thing I was responsible for' brings us to another aspect of his persona – the 'outsider/insider'. This was partly a by-product of the smallness of Irish society, but was also the result of the 'outsiders' with whom he shared a republican past seizing state power. The marginalization of republicans in the immediate post-Civil War years, on top of the colonial experience, created an enduring 'anti-establishment', 'outsider' self-regard, even among those who became the establishment and the new elite, and it was this that O'Donnell tapped into. He retained a cheeky intimacy in public with de Valera and the upper echelons of Fianna Fáil, and a close personal friendship with many of them in private. As Richard English puts it, he was 'personably amicable yet unrepentantly dissident; involved with and yet apart from those at the heart of Irish influence'.[20] He saw no contradiction between his politics and his friendship with the powerful and the rich. He was friendly with wealthy businessmen such as J.P. Digby of Pye, Joseph McGrath of the Irish Sweepstakes and, of course, Tony O'Reilly. O'Donnell's relationship with the latter arose not from any shared history, but from the fact that he sent his adopted son to Belvedere College, the elite Catholic private school.

The failure of his overall socialist republican project to achieve its goals should not blind us to O'Donnell's many real achievements, most of which cannot be measured by conventional, state-centred criteria of political success. His trade union work, his campaigns on behalf of emigrants and small farmers, his involvement in the battle against the slums – all of these led to real and fundamental improvements in the lot of many ordinary people. His private generosity benefited many; his encouragement and ability to empower and inspire transformed the lives of countless writers and activists; and it is impossible to know how many people were influenced by his journalism and literature to view the world in a different way. O'Donnell's major conventional political success was his initiation and promotion of the campaign against the land annuities, which ultimately influenced the course of Irish history when it was taken up by Fianna Fáil.

His range of talents, his involvement in so many areas of Irish life over most of the twentieth century, and the ambiguity of his political legacy have led to a situation whereby 'everyone in Ireland has his own Peadar O'Donnell'.[21] Historically and politically, those of his critics who are opposed to republicanism, socialism and/or socialist republicanism can use him as a hook on which to hang their hostility to all or some of those philosophies and movements; militant non-socialist republicans can dismiss him as an eccentric; the CPI can celebrate the best member it never had; revolutionary socialists and social democrats can use him to symbolize the failures of the Irish left from their respective positions.[22] Ultimately, however, as O'Donnell himself tried to show in his fiction, the fate of the individual must always be viewed through the widest possible lens. In this sense, and judged by the standards of the socialist and republican ideals that he himself cherished, the political life of Peadar O'Donnell is less the story of a lost revolutionary, perhaps, than of a lost revolution.

Notes and references

Abbreviations

AP	*An Phoblacht*
D/FA	Department of Foreign Affairs
D/IC	Department of Industry and Commerce
D/J	Department of Justice
D/T	Department of An Taoiseach
GFO	*The Gates Flew Open*
ILHMA	Irish Labour History Museum and Archive, Dublin
IMA	Irish Military Archives, Dublin
NAI	National Archives of Ireland, Dublin
NLI	National Library of Ireland, Dublin
RTsKhIDNI	Russian Centre for the Conservation and Study of Documents of Modern History, Moscow
TWBAD	*There Will Be Another Day*
UCDAD	University College Dublin, Archives Department

Introduction

1 O'Donnell speech to the Patrick MacGill Summer School, August 1985 (thanks to Richard McClafferty and Peter Hegarty); Peadar O'Donnell, *Salud! An Irishman in Spain* (Methuen, London, 1937), p. 225.

2 J. Bowyer Bell, *The Secret Army: The IRA* (Poolbeg, Dublin, 1998 edn), p. 85.

3 *Monkeys in the Superstructure: Reminiscences of Peadar O'Donnell* (Salmon, Galway, 1986), p. 30.

4 O'Donnell to Jonathan Cape, 24 February 1933, Jonathan Cape Archives, University of Reading.

5 Grattan Freyer, *Peadar O'Donnell* (Bucknell University Press, Lewisburg, 1973); Michael McInerney, *Peadar O'Donnell: Irish Social Rebel* (The O'Brien

Press, Dublin, 1974); Peter Hegarty, *Peadar O'Donnell* (Mercier Press, Cork, 1999).

6   Belfast speech, 7 April 1984, cited by Richard English, *Radicals and the Republic: Socialist Republicanism in the Irish Free State 1925–1937* (Clarendon Press, Oxford, 1994), p. 256.
7   O'Donnell in *The Banner* (ICND journal), vol. 1, no. 1, June 1963.
8   Benedict Kiely, 'A Sort of Rory of the Hill: Peadar O'Donnell', unpublished MS, 1995.

1: 'Let us become rebels' 1893–1921

Title quote: O'Donnell speech to Letterkenny INTO, *Derry Journal*, 13 February 1919.

1   McInerney, p. 33. O'Donnell celebrated his birthday on 22 February, though his birth certificate records his birth date as 12 March (Office of the Registrar General, Dublin). The general information for this section comes from: McInerney; Freyer; Hegarty; 'I Remember, I Remember', RTÉ Radio, 1 September 1976; Joe Mulholland interview with Peadar O'Donnell, August 1985, broadcast on RTÉ television, 9 October 1986 and the *Census of Ireland*, 1901 and 1911.
2   O'Donnell interview, *Sunday Independent*, 1 July 1979.
3   'I Remember, I Remember'; McInerney, p. 35.
4   Peadar O'Donnell, *The Gates Flew Open* (Mercier Press, Cork, 1966 edn), p. 93; Patrick Bolger, *The Irish Co-operative Movement: Its History and Development* (Institute of Public Administration, Dublin, 1977), pp. 241–2.
5   D.R. O'Connor-Lysaght interview with Peadar O'Donnell, 23 February 1983, ILHMA; Hegarty, pp. 24–5 and 48.
6   Joe McGarrigle, *Donegal Profiles* (Donegal Democrat, Ballyshannon, 1986), p. 185.
7   Hegarty, p. 23.
8   McInerney, p. 36; Peadar O'Donnell, 'The Irish in Britain', *The Bell*, vol. 6, no. 5, August 1943.
9   O'Connor-Lysaght interview with O'Donnell, 23 February 1983.
10 McInerney, p. 36.
11 Uinseann MacEoin, *Survivors* (Argenta, Dublin, 1980), p. 22; McInerney, p. 36; Hegarty, pp. 26–8.
12 Peadar O'Donnell, *There Will Be Another Day* (Dolmen Press, Dublin, 1963), pp. 66–8.
13 Anton McCabe, '"The Stormy Petrel of the Transport Workers": Peadar O'Donnell, Trade Unionist, 1917–1920', *Saothar* 19, 1994, p. 41.
14 MacEoin, *Survivors*, pp. 21–2; Freyer, p. 24.
15 *Derry Journal*, 21 February 1919, cited in McCabe, 'Stormy Petrel', p. 42.
16 O'Connor-Lysaght interview with O'Donnell, 23 February 1983; MacGill Summer School speech; McCabe, 'Stormy Petrel', pp. 41–2.
17 *Derry Journal*, 13 February 1918, cited in McCabe, 'Stormy Petrel', p. 42.
18 Anne O'Dowd, *Spalpeens and Tattie Hokers: The History and Folklore of the Irish*

Migratory Agricultural Worker in Ireland and Britain (Irish Academic Press, Dublin, 1991), pp. 190–2; C. Desmond Greaves, *The Irish Transport and General Workers' Union: The Formative Years, 1909–1923* (Gill and Macmillan, Dublin, 1982), pp. 203–4; O'Connor-Lysaght interview with O'Donnell, 23 February 1983; McCabe, 'Stormy Petrel', p. 43.

19 Hegarty, p. 68.
20 McInerney, p. 37; *Monkeys*, p. 9; O'Connor-Lysaght interview with O'Donnell, 23 February 1983.
21 McInerney, p. 38; McCabe, 'Stormy Petrel', p. 43.
22 *Voice of Labour*, 1 February 1919.
23 MacGill Summer School speech; Mulholland interview with O'Donnell (1985), RTÉ television, 9 October, 1986.
24 O'Connor-Lysaght interview with O'Donnell, 23 February 1983; MacGill Summer School speech; McInerney, pp. 38–40; Mike Milotte, *Communism in Modern Ireland: The Pursuit of the Workers' Republic since 1916* (Gill and Macmillan, Dublin, 1984), pp. 24–37.
25 Greaves, *ITGWU*, p. 232; Emmet O'Connor, 'War and Syndicalism 1914–1923' in Donal Nevin (ed.), *Trade Union Century* (Mercier Press, Cork, 1994), p. 59.
26 McCabe, 'Stormy Petrel', pp. 43–5; Conor Kostick, *Revolution in Ireland: Popular Militancy 1917 to 1923* (Pluto Press, London, 1996), p. 70; *Monkeys*, pp. 11–14; Hegarty, pp. 48–52; Lord French to War Cabinet, 7 February 1919, quoted by Emmet O'Connor, *Syndicalism in Ireland, 1917–1923* (Cork University Press, Cork, 1988), p. 71.
27 McCabe, 'Stormy Petrel', pp. 45–6; Greaves, *ITGWU*, p. 232; *Monkeys*, pp. 15–17.
28 MacGill Summer School speech.
29 Hegarty, p. 64.
30 Ibid., pp. 60–5; Greaves, *ITGWU*, p. 281.
31 *Voice of Labour*, 25 October 1919.
32 McCabe, 'Stormy Petrel', p. 46.
33 Emmet O'Connor, *A Labour History of Ireland 1824–1960* (Gill and Macmillan, Dublin, 1992), p. 101.
34 O'Connor, *Syndicalism*, pp. 174–5.
35 McCabe, 'Stormy Petrel', p. 47.
36 Ibid., p. 48.
37 Ibid., pp. 47–8; O'Connor-Lysaght interview with O'Donnell, 23 February 1983.
38 Hegarty, pp. 72–7; McInerney, p. 39; O'Connor-Lysaght interview with O'Donnell, 23 February 1983.
39 *Londonderry Sentinel*, 23 November 1920, cited in McCabe, 'Stormy Petrel', p. 47.
40 O'Connor, *Syndicalism*, p. 174.
41 McCabe, 'Stormy Petrel', p. 48.
42 Seamus McCann statement, 'Operations carried out by the IRA which I

took part in, against British Crown Forces 1918–11 July 1921', Letterkenny, 12 December 1952. (Copy kindly supplied by Peter Hegarty.)

43   McCann statement; Hegarty, pp. 80–4.
44   O'Donnell in conversation with Joe Sweeney and Ernie O'Malley, 3 June 1949, O'Malley notebooks, O'Malley Papers, P17b/98, UCDAD.
45   Hegarty, pp. 86–90.
46   Ibid., pp. 91–3.
47   *TWBAD*, pp. 19–20; MacEoin, *Survivors*, p. 25.
48   O'Connor-Lysaght interview with O'Donnell, 23 February 1983.

2: 'I'm in the wrong war!' 1921–1925

Title quote: O'Donnell to Liam Mellows, 28 June 1922, recounted by O'Donnell in Mulholland interview (1985), RTÉ television, 9 October 1986.

1   MacEoin, *Survivors*, p. 24.
2   C.S. Andrews, *Dublin Made Me: An Autobiography* (Mercier Press, Dublin and Cork, 1979), pp. 196–200.
3   *Derry Journal*, 18 November 1921.
4   E. Rumpf and A.C. Hepburn, *Nationalism and Socialism in Twentieth-Century Ireland* (Liverpool University Press, Liverpool, 1977), p. 35.
5   Peadar O'Donnell, 'The Irish Struggle To-day', *Left Review*, 2 April 1936, p. 298.
6   *GFO*, p. 17.
7   'Irish Struggle', p. 298.
8   'O'Donnell Remembers', *Irish Times*, 22 February 1983; O'Connor, *Syndicalism*, p. 148.
9   O'Connor-Lysaght interview with O'Donnell, 23 February 1983; *Workers' Republic*, 25 November 1922 and 25 August 1923.
10   See Tom Garvin, *Nationalist Revolutionaries in Ireland 1858–1928* (Doubleday, New York, 1987), pp. 141–9, and Rumpf and Hepburn, pp. 34–6.
11   Dorothy MacArdle, *The Irish Republic* (Irish Press Publications, Dublin, 1951), pp. 673–9; Bowyer Bell, pp. 32–3; Hegarty, pp. 103–4.
12   MacArdle, pp. 694–8; Hegarty, p. 104; Ernie O'Malley, *The Singing Flame* (Anvil Books, Dublin, 1978), pp. 75–6.
13   MacGill Summer School speech; McInerney, p. 44; O'Donnell, *Not Yet Emmet* (New Books, Dublin, n.d.[1985]), p. 15; MacEoin, *Survivors*, pp. 24–5. O'Donnell admitted his part in this shambles, frequently using 'we' in his criticisms.
14   MacEoin, *Survivors*, p. 25.
15   This account is based on MacArdle, pp. 706–44.
16   Mulholland interview with O'Donnell (1985), RTÉ television, 9 October 1986.
17   *GFO*, p. 17.
18   *GFO*, pp. 14–17; Greaves, p. 362.
19   *Workers' Republic*, 22 and 29 July 1922.

20 Ibid, 22, 29 July 1922 and 12 August 1922; Milotte, pp. 59–61; 'Roddy Connolly: 60 years of political activity', *Irish Times*, 27 August 1976.
21 Michael Hopkinson, *Green Against Green: The Irish Civil War* (Gill and Macmillan, Dublin, 1988), p. 186.
22 O'Donnell interview with Angela Crean, 9 April 1985, cited in Richard English, *Radicals and the Republic*, p. 55, n. 244.
23 *GFO*, p. 25.
24 Ibid., pp. 24–32.
25 MacArdle, p. 804.
26 *GFO*, pp. 22–4; Peter Hegarty interview with Peadar Joe O'Donnell, 1998.
27 Hopkinson, pp. 186–8; C. Desmond Greaves, *Liam Mellows and the Irish Revolution* (Lawrence and Wishart, London, 1971), pp. 379–81.
28 *GFO*, pp. 34–6.
29 Hopkinson, pp. 190–1.
30 MacEoin, *Survivors*, p. 29.
31 Ibid., p. 41.
32 *Workers Republic*, 23 December 1922 to 3 February 1923; Milotte, pp. 63–5.
33 Hopkinson, p. 228; *GFO*, pp. 44–53; Hegarty, p. 137.
34 *GFO*, pp. 54–66.
35 Ibid., pp. 68–9; MacEoin, *Survivors*, p. 30; Hegarty, p. 140.
36 *GFO*, pp. 74–5.
37 Ibid., p. 75.
38 *Workers' Republic*, 25 August 1923; *Irish Times*, 22 and 24 August 1923.
39 O'Connor-Lysaght interview with O'Donnell, 23 February 1983.
40 *GFO*, p. 80.
41 Ibid., p. 86.
42 Ibid., pp. 89–90.
43 Ibid., p. 93.
44 Ibid., p. 94.
45 Ibid., p. 97.
46 O'Malley to Childers, 28 November 1923, in Richard English and Cormac O'Malley (eds), *Prisoners: The Civil War Letters of Ernie O'Malley* (Poolbeg, Dublin, 1991), p. 99.
47 Hopkinson, pp. 270–1.
48 Hegarty, p. 151.
49 Ibid.; *GFO*, pp. 104–6; MacGill Summer School speech.
50 Marriage entry of Peadar O'Donnell and Lile O'Donel, Office of the Registrar General, Dublin.
51 Peadar Joe O'Donnell interview, 1998.
52 Cormac O'Malley interview with O'Donnell and George Gilmore, October 1970, cited in Richard English, *Radicals and the Republic*, p. 64; O'Donnell letter to Denis Johnson (n.d. given), cited by Hegarty, p. 156; Tim Pat Coogan, *The IRA* (Pall Mall, London, 1970), p. 67.

53   Peter Pyne, 'The Third Sinn Féin Party: 1923–1926', *The Economic and Social Review*, vol. 1, no. 1, October 1969, pp. 32–40.
54   O'Donnell to Twomey, 8 June 1924, Moss Twomey Papers, P69/43/65, UCDAD.
55   *The Economic Programme of Sinn Féin* (1924), cited in English, *Radicals and the Republic*, p. 65.
56   Minutes of 7–8 August 1924 meetings of Comhairle na dTeachtaí and Second Dáil, reproduced in J. Anthony Gaughan, *Austin Stack: Portrait of a Separatist* (Kingdom Books, Dublin, 1977), Addendum, pp. 317–59.
57   *TWBAD*, p. 35.
58   Gaughan, pp. 334–6.
59   Pyne, 'Sinn Féin', pp. 40–3.
60   De Valera to Joseph McGarrity, 13 March 1926, McGarrity Papers, MS 17,441, NLI.
61   Paul Bew, Ellen Hazelkorn and Henry Patterson, *The Dynamics of Irish Politics* (Lawrence and Wishart, London, 1989), pp. 28–9.
62   Milotte, pp. 67–77; Emmet O'Connor, 'Jim Larkin and the Communist Internationals, 1923–9', *Irish Historical Studies*, xxxi, no. 123, May 1999, pp. 358–60.
63   Barry McLoughlin and Emmet O'Connor, 'Sources on Ireland and the Communist International', *Saothar* 21, 1996, p. 106; O'Connor, 'Larkin', pp. 360–1; Milotte, pp. 67–73.
64   Milotte, pp. 77–9; O'Connor, 'Larkin', pp. 363–4.
65   The Earl of Longford and Thomas P. O'Neill, *Eamon de Valera* (Houghton Mifflin, Boston, 1971), p. 240.
66   Pyne, 'Sinn Féin', p. 43.
67   *TWBAD*, p. 35.
68   English, *Radicals and the Republic*, pp. 66–8; Bowyer Bell, p. 52; Uinseann MacEoin, *The IRA in the Twilight Years 1923–1948* (Argenta, Dublin, 1997), p. 121.
69   *Report of General Army Convention*, November 1925, cited in English, *Radicals and the Republic*, p. 68.
70   *TWBAD*, pp. 35–6.
71   *TWBAD*, pp. 35–6; Bowyer Bell, pp. 52–3.
72   O'Connor-Lysaght interview with O'Donnell, 23 February 1983.

3: 'My pen is a weapon' 1926–1931

Title quote: O'Donnell to Jonathan Cape, 24 February 1933, Cape Archives, University of Reading.
1   Pyne, 'Sinn Féin', pp. 44–7; *AP*, 16 April 1926.
2   *AP*, 16 and 23 April 1926; *TWBAD*, p. 36.
3   RTÉ interview, February 1983, rebroadcast on 13 May 1986.
4   The best treatment of *An Phoblacht*, and the republican press generally in the 1920s and 1930s, is to be found in James P. McHugh, 'Voices of the Rearguard – A Study of *An Phoblacht*: Irish Republican Thought in the Post-Revolutionary Era, 1923–37' (MA thesis, UCD, 1983).

5   Deirdre McMahon, *Republicans and Imperialists: Anglo-Irish Relations in the 1930s* (Yale University Press, New Haven, 1984), pp. 38–9; MacEoin, *Twilight Years*, p. 133.

6   *AP*, 4 June, 9 July, 23 July 1926.

7   *AP*, 3 September 1926.

8   *TWBAD*, p. 34.

9   Ibid., pp. 30 and 38.

10   *AP*, 8 October 1926.

11   Ibid., 8 April 1927.

12   *Irish World*, 7 May 1927, quoted in Margaret Ward, *Hanna Sheehy Skeffington: A Life* (Attic Press, Cork, 1997), p. 286.

13   *AP*, 15 April 1927; *TWBAD*, pp. 55–6.

14   O'Flaherty to Garnett, 30 May 1927, in A.A. Kelly (ed.), *The Letters of Liam O'Flaherty* (Wolfhound Press, Dublin, 1996), pp. 184–5.

15   O'Flaherty to Cape, 21 June 1927, Ibid., p. 188.

16   See inscription, *Adrigoole* (Jonathan Cape, London, 1929).

17   Quoted in Henry Patterson, *The Politics of Illusion: A Political History of the IRA* (Serif, London, 1997), p. 43.

18   *AP*, 24 June and 10 September 1927.

19   *AP*, 1 October–3 December 1927; quote from the issue of 12 November 1927.

20   Bowyer Bell, p. 65.

21   *TWBAD*, p. 79.

22   Ibid., p. 85.

23   *Monkeys*, pp. 25–6; MacEoin, *Survivors*, p. 33; O'Donnell interview with Richard Dunphy cited in Richard Dunphy, *The Making of Fianna Fáil Power in Ireland 1923–1948* (Clarendon Press, Oxford, 1995), p. 97.

24   *AP*, 11 February 1928.

25   'Report submitted to Government by Department of Justice on Alliance between Irish Republican Army and Communists', D/T S 5864 (A), Appendix I, NAI.

26   See Maurice Moore Papers, MS 10,560, NLI.

27   O'Connor, 'Larkin', pp. 365–7.

28   See Barry McLoughlin, 'Proletarian Academics or Party Functionaries? Irish Communists at the International Lenin School, Moscow, 1927–1937', *Saothar* 22, 1997, pp. 63–79.

29   John Callaghan, 'The Communists and the Colonies: Anti-Imperialism between the Wars', in Geoff Andrews, Nina Fishman and Kevin Morgan (eds), *Opening the Books: Essays on the Social and Cultural History of British Communism* (Pluto Press, London, 1995), pp. 7–18.

30   D/J 'Notes on Communism in Saorstát Éireann', 1936, D/J (Security Division) Box 4/202, NAI.

31   Garda report on 4 October 1928 Mansion House meeting, D/J 8/682, NAI; *AP*, 23 February 1929; 'Notes on Communism in Saorstát Éireann', Supplement, p. 5, D/J Box 4/202, NAI.

32   Garda report on LAI Congress, Frankfurt-on-Main, 16 September 1929, D/J JUS 8/682, NAI.

33   D/J, Ibid.; Milotte, p. 93; James Hogan, *Could Ireland become Communist? The Facts of the Case* (Cahill, Dublin, 1935), p. 37; O'Connor, 'Larkin', p. 367.

34   *AP*, 13 July 1929; Conor Foley, *Legion of the Rearguard: The IRA and the Modern Irish State* (Pluto Press, London, 1992), p. 81.

35   Milotte, pp. 102–3.

36   McHugh, pp. 494–7.

37   Patterson, p. 53.

38   *AP*, 18 May and 7 December 1929 and 1 March 1930.

39   Ibid., 28 June 1928.

40   *Dáil Debates*, vol. 24, cols. 1888–1902.

41   Ibid.

42   Ibid., cols. 2057–9.

43   Ibid., vol. 28, cols. 1883–6.

44   English, *Radicals and the Republic*, p. 109.

45   It was due for publication in the autumn of 1927, and 1927 remained its original publication date, though it appears not to have become available until early 1928.

46   O'Flaherty to May O'Callaghan, 29 January 1928 in Kelly, *Letters*, p. 211.

47   *AP*, 28 January, 11 February and 3 March 1928.

48   Benedict Kiely, 'A Sort of Rory of the Hill'.

49   *TWBAD*, pp. 24–5.

50   *Adrigoole*, pp. 266, 268 and 314.

51   *AP*, 3 August 1929.

52   *The Irish Book Lover*, xvii, September–October 1929, pp. 110–11.

53   Alexander Gonzalez, *Peadar O' Donnell: A Readers' Guide* (Dufour Editions, Chester Springs, 1997), pp. 23–8; Mary Carden, 'The Literary Achievement of Peadar O'Donnell' (MA thesis, UCD, 1973), p. 204.

54   Sean O'Faolain, *The Irish* (Penguin, Middlesex, 1969 edn), p. 130.

55   *AP*, 22 November and 6 December 1930.

56   *Irish Book Lover*, xviii, September–October 1930, pp. 137–8.

57   Gonzalez, pp. 39–43.

58   Freyer, pp. 47–8.

59   *AP*, 13 December 1930.

60   *GFO*, p. 24.

61   A Department of Justice memorandum for the government stated that 'O'Donnell is openly anti-clerical: his last book 'The Knife' condemns in the strongest possible terms the influence of the Church, particularly the Bishops, on Irish political development.' (Report Submitted to Government by D/J on 'Alliance between Irish Republican Army and Communists' (1931), Appendix I, D/T, S 5864 (A), NAI.)

62   *AP*, 22 February 1930.

63   D/J 'Notes on Communism', p. 14.

64   *AP*, 1 and 8 February 1930.

65 D/J 'Notes on Communism', pp. 14–15; D/J memo, 19 March 1930, and 'Revolutionary Organisations' memo, 4 April 1930, in D/T S5074 A and B; 'Workers' Revolutionary Party', Garda report to Secretary, Department of Justice, 13 June 1930, D/J 8/691, NAI.

66 *AP*, 5 April 1930; 'Communist Activities in Saorstát Éireann, 1929–30, D/J memo 27 March 1930 – 'Peasant Farmers Organisation (Kristertern [*sic*])', D/T S 5074A, NAI.

67 See O'Donnell, *Plan of Campaign for Irish Working Farmers* (Fodhla, Dublin, 1931), *passim*.

68 Hogan, pp. 89–90.

69 *Workers' Voice*, 28 June 1930.

70 Ibid.; *AP*, 5 and 12 April 1930; *Monkeys*, p. 23; Hogan, pp. 89–90.

71 *AP*, 19 July 1930.

72 Ibid., 19 April 1930.

73 Ibid., 12 April 1930; text of ECCI letter, D/J 'Notes on Communism', Appendix III.

74 *AP*, 9 July 1930.

75 *Workers' Voice*, 30 August 1930.

76 *AP*, 9 July 1930; Milotte, pp. 99–100; *AP*, 14 June 1930; Garda report on LAI meeting, 25 September 1930, D/J 8/682, NAI.

77 MacEoin, *Survivors*, p. 122.

78 *AP*, 18 October and 15 November 1930.

79 Ibid., 29 November 1930–28 March 1931.

80 Ibid., 7 February 1931.

81 *Plan of Campaign, passim.*

82 O'Donnell to EPC Secretary, 20 December 1932, RTsKhIDNI, 495/89/85/17A; *AP*, 9, 16 May and 4 July 1931.

83 *AP*, July–September 1931; Jonathan Hammill, 'Saor Éire and the IRA: An Exercise in Deception?', *Saothar* 20, 1995, p. 58; Bowyer Bell, p. 82; MacEoin, *Survivors,* p. 6, and *Twilight Years*, p. 620; Ronnie Munck and Bill Rolston, *Belfast in the Thirties: An Oral History* (Blackstaff Press, Belfast 1987), p. 172.

84 Dunphy, pp. 74–5.

85 D/J 'Report on the present position' (August 1931), D/T S5864B, NAI.

86 *TWBAD*, p. 121; *AP*, 11 April 1931.

87 *AP*, 27 June 1931; Patterson, p. 56; D/J, 'Report'; *TWBAD*, pp. 121–6.

88 D/J 'Alliance'.

89 Patrick Murray, *Oracles of God: The Roman Catholic Church and Irish Politics, 1922–37* (UCD Press, Dublin, 2000), pp. 320–1; Cosgrave to MacRory, 11 September 1931, D/T S5864B, NAI.

90 *AP*, 3 October 1931; Bowyer Bell, pp. 87 and 96; Saor Éire 'Constitution and Rules', D/T S5864B, NAI; 'Saor Éire . . . Three Resolutions Adopted by First National Congress', NLI.

91 *AP*, 17 October 1931; *Dáil Debates*, vol. 40, col. 113, 14 October 1931.

92 Hammill, p. 62; Milotte, pp. 100 and 107.

93 Summary of opening statement by Cosgrave in the Dáil, 14 October 1931, and text of the joint pastoral, D/T S2267, NAI; *Dáil Debates*, vol. 40, cols 104–13, 14 October 1931.
94 Dermot Keogh, 'De Valera, the Catholic Church and the 'Red Scare', 1931–1932', in J.P. O'Carroll and John A. Murphy (eds), *De Valera and his Times* (Cork University Press, Cork, 1986), pp. 140–2.
95 Mary Banta, 'The Red Scare in the Irish Free State' (MA thesis, UCD, 1982), p. 45.
96 O'Donnell to Jonathan Cape, 23 February 1933 and to Ruth Atkinson at Cape, 21 June 1933, Jonathan Cape Archives, University of Reading.
97 *TWBAD*, p. 129.

4: 'Bridgeheads of hope' 1932–1939

Title quote: O'Donnell phrase quoted in James McDyer, *Fr McDyer of Glencolumbkille: An Autobiography* (Brandon Books, Dingle, 1982), p. 84.

1   *TWBAD*, p. 127.
2   Patterson, p. 61.
3   Ibid.; Keogh, 'De Valera', pp. 144–57; Dunphy, pp. 142–4.
4   IRA GHQ to Commanders of Independent Units, 12 January 1932, D/T, S5864C, NAI.
5   *TWBAD*, p. 131; Foley, pp. 100–1.
6   Ibid.
7   9 February 1932, copy in RTsKhIDNI, 495/89/85/1.
8   Vincent Browne (ed.), *The Magill Book of Irish Politics* (Magill Publications, Dublin, 1981), pp. 112 and 115; Dunphy, p. 144.
9   Peadar O'Donnell, *The Bothy Fire and All That* (Irish People Publications, Dublin, 1937), p. 9.
10 George Gilmore, *The Irish Republican Congress* (Cork Workers' Club, Cork, 1978 edn), p. 6.
11 *Republican Congress*, 11 August 1934; Bowyer Bell, pp. 101–2.
12 *AP*, 2 April 1932.
13 *Republican Congress*, 11 August 1934.
14 Gilmore to Twomey, September 1932, Moss Twomey Papers, P 69/53, UCDAD.
15 Quoted in Garvin, p. 127.
16 Peadar O'Donnell, 'The Clergy and me', *Doctrine and Life*, vol. 24, no. 10, October 1974, p. 541.
17 *Irish Times*, 14 June 1932; *AP*, 16 June 1932.
18 *Irish Times*, 15 June 1932.
19 Ibid., 16 June 1932.
20 *AP*, 9 and 16 July 1932; *Irish Independent*, 20 July 1932.
21 Julia Carlson, *Banned in Ireland: Censorship and the Irish Writer* (Routledge, London, 1990), pp. 7–8; Brian Fallon, *An Age of Innocence: Irish Culture 1930–1960* (Gill and Macmillan, Dublin, 1998), pp. 45–6; Freyer, p. 106.

22 Peadar O'Donnell, *Salud! An Irishman in Spain* (Methuen, London, 1937), pp. 7–14.
23 Ibid.; O'Donnell interview, *Sunday Independent*, 1 July 1979; McInerney, p. 103.
24 Shiela McHugh, 'Peadar O'Donnell – The Achill Conection', paper delivered at the 'Peadar O'Donnell Weekend', Dungloe, Co. Donegal, 20–22 October 2000; Hegarty, p. 215.
25 Banta, p. 79.
26 *Irish Workers' Voice*, 5 November 1932.
27 Patrick Byrne, *The Irish Republican Congress Revisited* (Connolly Association, London, 1994 edn), p. 27.
28 Milotte, pp. 128–38.
29 *AP*, 16 July 1932; Brian Hanly, 'Catholic Defenders or Republicans? The IRA in 1930s Northern Ireland', unpublished paper, 1999.
30 Munck and Rolston, pp. 183–4.
31 Banta, pp. 105–6; *AP*, 25 June, 2 July 1932; McMahon, p. 84; O'Donnell to EPC Secretary, 20 December 1932, RTsKhIDNI, 495/89/85/17–17A.
32 Finance memo for the cabinet, 11 November 1932, D/T S2888, NAI.
33 Banta, pp. 105–6; Bew et al., pp. 44–7.
34 O'Donnell to EPC Secretary, 20 December 1932, RTsKhIDNI, 495/89/85/17–17A.
35 Ibid.
36 O'Donnell to EPC Secretary, 4 January and 16 January 1933, RTsKhIDNI, 495/89/94/1–5.
37 *AP*, 21 January 1933.
38 Peadar O'Donnell, 'Introduction' in Brian O'Neill, *The War for the Land in Ireland* (Martin Lawrence, London, 1933), pp. 11–12.
39 O'Donnell to EPC Secretary, 28 December 1933, RTsKhIDNI, 495/89/94/13; Tim Rees and Andrew Thorpe (eds), 'Introduction', *International Communism and the Communist International 1919–43* (Manchester University Press, Manchester, 1998), p. 2.
40 Pat Feeley, *The Gralton Affair* (Coolock Free Press, Dublin, 1986), *passim*.
41 Ibid., p. 47.
42 Ibid., pp. 43–66; *Salud!*, pp. 76–7.
43 Banta, pp. 131–51; Garda report, 29 March 1933, and Garda Commissioner to Secretary, Justice, 30 March 1933, 'Anti-communist demonstrations 1933', D/J 8/711, NAI.
44 Milotte, pp. 141–3; Stephen Bowler, 'Sean Murray, 1898–1961, and the Pursuit of Stalinism in One Country', *Saothar* 18, 1993, pp. 44–5; *AP*, 17 June 1933; *Irish Workers' Voice*, 24 June 1933.
45 'Constitution and Governmental Programme for the Republic of Ireland: adopted by the GAC of Óglaigh na hÉireann, March 1933', Coyle O'Donnell Papers, P61/11 (1), UCDAD; Gilmore, p. 29; 'The Irish Struggle To-day', p. 299; Minutes of the General Army Convention, 17 March

1934, Sean MacEntee papers, P67/525, UCDAD; Sean Cronin, *Frank Ryan: The Search for the Republic* (Repsol, Dublin, 1980), p. 46.

46 O'Donnell to EPC Secretary, 14 August 1933, and reply, 8 September 1933, RTsKhIDNI, 495/89/94/11–12; Milotte, pp. 145–6.

47 O'Donnell to EPC Secretary, 14 August 1933, and reply, 8 September 1933, RTsKhIDNI, 495/89/94/11–12.

48 Milotte, p. 148; Garda report on Irish Labour Defence League, 28 February 1934, D/J 8/338, NAI.

49 Minutes of the General Army Convention; 'Irish Struggle', p. 299; Gilmore, pp. 29–30; D/J 'Notes on the Republican Congress Movement', 1936, D/J Security Division, Box 4/202, NAI; Bowyer Bell, pp. 112–13.

50 Minutes of meeting between O'Donnell, Price and the Cumann na mBan executive, 20 April 1934, Sighle Humphreys Papers, P106/2040, UCDAD; D/J 'Notes on Republican Congress'; Gilmore, pp. 30–1; Byrne, p. 13; *AP*, 14 April 1934.

51 *AP*, 21 April 1934; O'Donnell letter to *Irish Press* re army council statement, n.d. [April 1934], Humphreys Papers, P106/1488, UCDAD; D/J 'Notes'; *Republican Congress*, 5 May 1934.

52 *Republican Congress*, 5 May 1934.

53 Gilmore, p. 44; *Republican Congress*, 23 June 1934.

54 Nora Connolly O'Brien and Peter Carelton in MacEoin, *Survivors*, pp. 213 and 308; Byrne, p. 15; *Irish Citizen Army Bulletin*, 20 November 1934; Price to Sighle Humphreys, 13 July 1934, Humphreys Papers, P106/1489, UCDAD; Roddy Connolly to all ranks, 17 November 1934, JUS 8/320, 'Irish Citizen Army (1934)', NAI.

55 *Republican Congress*, 5 and 19 May 1934; D/J 'Notes'; Byrne, pp. 17 and 21–2; Garda report 2 June 1934, D/J 8/339, 'Irish Unemployed Workers' Movement', NAI.

56 Gilmore, pp. 40–4; Cronin, p. 36; Byrne, pp. 17–20; D/J 'Notes'; *Republican Congress, passim*; Banta, pp. 272–3.

57 *Republican Congress*, 4 and 11 August 1934; Gilmore, pp. 44–5; *Irish Workers Voice*, 1 September 1934.

58 *Republican Congress*, 6 and 13 October 1934; Gilmore, pp. 45–51; Byrne, pp. 30–2; 'Irish Struggle', p. 299; Hogan, p. 129.

59 *Republican Congress*, 6 October 1934.

60 Gilmore, p. 54.

61 *AP*, 13 October 1934.

62 *Citizen Army Bulletin*, 20 and 27 November 1934; Connolly to all ranks, 17 and 20 November, D/J 8/320, 'Irish Citizen Army (1934)', NAI; *Republican Congress*, 8 December 1934.

63 *Republican Congress*, October–November 1934; D/J 'Notes'; D/J 8/339, 'Irish Unemployed Workers' Movement', NAI; Milotte, p. 159; Gilmore, p. 40; Byrne, p. 15.

64 Peadar O'Donnell, *On the Edge of the Stream* (Jonathan Cape, London, 1934), pp. 208 and 213.

65 *Irish Press*, 17 November 1935; Benedict Kiely, 'A Sort of Rory of the Hill'.

66 Banta, pp. 204–5; *Monkeys*, p. 7.

67 *Irish Press*, 29 May and 4 June 1935.

68 E.M. Hogan, 'Biographical Sketch', and Brian Girvin, 'Nationalism, Catholicism and Democracy: Hogan's Intellectual Evolution', in Donnchadh O Corrain (ed.), *James Hogan: Revolutionary, Historian & Political Scientist* (Four Courts Press, Dublin, 2000), pp. 18–19 and 148; Hogan, p. 48; Hogan quoted in *Leinster Leader*, 1 September 1934, cited in Bew et al., pp. 64–5.

69 Milotte, 159–60; *Republican Congress*, 24 November 1934 and 30 March 1935; D/J 'Notes'.

70 Bowler, p. 47.

71 *Republican Congress*, 4 and 11 January 1936; D/J 'Notes'; Cronin, pp. 65 and 69.

72 *United Ireland*, 2 November 1935.

73 'Irish Struggle', p. 300.

74 Murray to the Anglo-American Secretariat of Comintern, n.d. [1935], RTsKhIDNI, 495/14/335/24.

75 Garda report, 14 April 1936, Sean MacEntee Papers, P67/526, UCDA; Byrne, pp. 33–4.

76 *Salud!*, pp. 8 and 14.

77 Ibid., pp. 7–9; Peadar O'Donnell, 'What I Saw in Spain', *Ireland To-Day*, vol. 1, no. 4, September 1936, p. 17.

78 *Salud!*, pp. 36, 40–78 and 123.

79 Ibid., pp. 99–125; 'What I Saw in Spain', p. 17.

80 See Fearghal McGarry, *Irish Politics and the Spanish Civil War* (Cork University Press, Cork, 1999), *passim*.

81 *Derry Journal*, 17 August 1936; *Irish Times*, 3 and 25 August 1936; Pete Jackson, 'A Rather One Sided Fight': the *Worker* and the Spanish Civil War', *Saothar* 23, 1998, pp. 82–3; *Irish Press*, 23 September 1936; 'What I Saw in Spain', p. 17.

82 *Derry Journal*, 17 August 1936.

83 'What I Saw in Spain', p. 17.

84 *Salud!*, p. 162.

85 Ibid., pp. 162–70; José Peritas, *Anarchists in the Spanish Revolution* (Freedom Press, London, 1990), p. 149; *AP*, 19 July 1930.

86 *Salud!*, pp. 196–9.

87 Ibid., pp. 186–7 and 207–9; Cronin, p. 152.

88 *Salud!*, p. 239.

89 McGarry, p. 80.

90 Frank Ryan to Gerald O'Reilly, 17 September 1936, in Sean Cronin, *Frank Ryan: The Search for the Republic* (Repsol, Dublin, 1980), p. 78.

91 *Irish Independent*, 7 November 1936; McGarry, pp. 99–100, quoting Joseph Walshe, Secretary, Department of External Affairs.

92 *Irish Democrat*, 8 May, 22 May and 5 June 1936; Ryan to Murray, 2 September 1937, quoted by Foley, p. 169; McGarry, pp. 69–70.

93 *Irish Democrat*, 5 June 1937; Gonzalez, p. 97; *Irish Book Lover*, xxv, 3, May–June 1937.

94 Cronin, p. 155.

95 McGarry, pp. 64 and 81; O'Connor-Lysaght interview with O'Donnell, 23 February 1983.

96 *AP*, 15 May 1937; *Irish Democrat*, 22 May 1937.

97 Bowyer Bell, pp. 139–46.

98 McHugh, 'The Achill Connection'; *Derry Journal*, 20 October 1937; Byrne, p. 41.

99 *Bothy Fire*, pp. 9–19.

100 See Dunphy, pp. 152–211.

101 *Gaelic American*, 10 June 1939.

102 Ibid., 10 and 17 June 1939.

103 *Irish Post*, 20 April, 1985, recounted by Donal O'Donovan, *Kevin Barry and His Time* (Glendale Press, Dublin, 1989), p. 191.

104 Peadar Joe O'Donnell interview, 1998; McInerney, p. 33; Margaret Mulvihill, *Charlotte Despard: A Biography* (Pandora, London, 1989), p. 193.

5: 'Somewhere out the road in history' 1940–1986

Title quote: O'Donnell in *The Banner* (ICND journal), vol. 1, no. 1, June 1963.

1 Peadar Joe O'Donnell interview, 1998; Freyer, p.88; Hegarty, pp. 225–6; Cronin, p. 109; James T. Farrell, *On Irish Themes* (Pennsylvania University Press, Philadelphia 1982), pp. 163–4; *TWBAD*, pp. 72–3; Honor Tracy, *Mind you, I've said nothing!: Forays in the Irish Republic* (Robert B. Luce, Washington DC, 1968), p. 56.

2 Peadar Joe O'Donnell interview, 1998; Hegarty, p. 226.

3 Derry Kelleher in MacEoin, *Twilight Years*, p. 640.

4 J.A. Belton to Frederick Boland, 20 December 1939, O'Donnell to Joseph Walshe, 22 December 1939, and copy of O'Donnell memo, D/FA (Sec) S113(a), NAI.

5 D/J, Office of Controller of Censorship, Monthly Reports, April 1940, NAI.

6 Freyer, p. 106.

7 'Invasion!', private source.

8 *Derry Journal*, 11 December 1940.

9 O'Donnell to L.A.W., New York, 3 June 1941, OCC 7/8, IMA.

10 Mulholland interview with O'Donnell (1985), RTÉ television, 9 October 1986; *The Bell*, vol. 13, no. 4, January 1947, p. 3.

11 McInerney, pp. 96–9.

12 John de Courcy Ireland, letter to *Saothar* 17, 1992, p. 12.

13 Dulanty to Walshe, 4 February 1944, including O'Donnell report (3 February 1944), and Boland to DEA, 22 August 1952, D/FA, 402/218,

NAI; Tracey Connolly, 'Irish Workers in Britain during World War Two', in Brian Girvin and Geoff Roberts (eds), *Ireland and the Second World War* (Four Courts Press, Dublin, 2000), p. 131; employment details from D/IC, E 194/45, NAI.

14 *Nusight*, September 1969, p. 79; Maurice Harmon, *Sean O'Faolain: A Life* (Constable, London, 1994), pp. 128–9.
15 *The Bell*, vol. 1, no. 1, October 1940, pp. 1–2.
16 Ibid., vol. 5, no. 3, December 1942, p. 208.
17 Michael O'Sullivan, *Brendan Behan: A Life* (Blackwater Press, Dublin, 1997), pp. 94–101; Anthony Cronin, *Dead as Doornails* (Lilliput Press, Dublin, 1999 edn), p. 72.
18 McInerney, p. 191.
19 O'Donnell interview, *Irish Press*, 10 January 1983.
20 'O'Donnell Salud!', *Hibernia*, 2 March 1973.
21 *The Bell*, vol. 17, no. 6, September 1951, p. 6; vol. 13, no. 4, January 1947, p. 2.
22 Ibid., vol. 12, no. 4, July 1946, p. 277; vol. 16, no. 2, November 1950, p. 6.
23 Ibid., vol. 14, no. 4, July 1947, pp. 1–2.
24 Ibid., vol. 13, no. 1, October 1946, pp. 4–5.
25 Ibid., vol. 19, no. 3, February 1954, p. 8.
26 Ibid., vol. 16, no. 6, March 1951, p. 7.
27 Anthony Cronin, *The Life of Riley* (Brandon Books, Dingle, 1983 edn), *passim*.
28 Tracy, pp. 56–7; Robert Greacan, *Brief Encounters: Literary Dublin and Belfast in the 1940s* (Cathair Books, Dublin, 1991), p. 31; Val Mulkern's notes on O'Donnell.
29 *The Bell*, vol. 16, no. 1, April 1948, pp. 1–3.
30 *Irish Times*, 25 February and 4 March 1970.
31 Richard Kearney, *Transitions: Narratives in Modern Irish Culture* (Wolfhound Press, Dublin, 1988), p. 263.
32 The government was comprised of Fine Gael, Labour, National Labour, Clann na Poblachta and Clann na Talmhan.
33 *Reports of the Commission on Emigration and Other Population Problems, 1948–1954* (Stationery Office, Dublin, 1954); 'Commission of Enquiry on Emigration and Rural Depopulation', D/T S 14249, NA; *Irish Press*, 22 April 1948; *Irish Times*, 13 July 1954.
34 *Reports*, p. 238.
35 Peadar O'Donnell, *The Big Windows* (The O'Brien Press, 1983 edn), *passim*; *Irish Times*, 2 July 1983; *Irish Press*, 18 June 1983; *Irish Independent*, 13 February 2000.
36 'Activities of Peadar O'Donnell in relation to the Irish Centre in London', D/FA (Sec), A 87, NAI.
37 Information from *Communist Party of Ireland: Outline History* (New Books, Dublin, n.d.), p. 59; John Cooney, *John Charles McQuaid: Ruler of Catholic Ireland* (The O'Brien Press, Dublin, 1999), pp. 321 and 488; Milotte, p. 228;

Irish Times, 14 May 1957 and 24 October 1964; 'O'Donnell Remembers', *Irish Times*, 22 February 1983.

38   *Challenge: A Journal of the Worker-Small Farmer Alliance*, vol. 1, no. 3, February 1968, p. 10.

39   Richard S. Harrison, *Irish Anti-War Movements 1824–1974* (Irish Peace Publications, Dublin, 1986), pp. 53–71; materials relating to ICND, John de Courcy Ireland Papers P29/a/113, P29/c/1–3, UCDAD.

40   'Anti-Apartheid Movement', D/FA (Sec), A 55/10, NAI.

41   D/FA 'Memorandum for the Information of the Government on Irish Appeals on the Situation in Vietnam', 1 January 1968, D/J 99/1/443, NAI; Vietnam material in de Courcy Ireland Papers, P29/c/4, P29/c/64a, UCDAD; *Irish Times*, 11 November 1969.

42   Vincent Tucker, 'State and Community: A Case Study of Glencolumbcille', in Chris Curtin and Thomas Wilson (eds), *Ireland from Below: Social Change and Local Communities* (Galway University Press, Galway, 1989), pp. 285–97; James McDyer, *Fr McDyer of Glencolumbkille: An Autobiography* (Brandon Books, Dingle, 1982), pp. 78–86; Tony Varley and Chris Curtin, 'Defending Rural Interests Against Nationalists in Twentieth Century Ireland: A Tale of Three Movements', pre-publication MS, p. 31 (since published in John Davis (ed.), *Rural Change in Ireland* (Institute of Irish Studies, Belfast, 1999)).

43   *Challenge*, vol. 1, no. 11, p. 9.

44   Peadar O'Donnell, *The Role of Industrial Workers in the Problems of the West* (The Kerryman, Tralee, n.d. [1966]), pp. 6–8.

45   Ivan Fallon, *The Player: The Life of Tony O'Reilly* (Coronet, London, 1994), p. 151.

46   Ibid., pp. 118–55; Fintan O'Toole, 'Tony O'Reilly and the News From Nowhere', in *The Ex-Isle of Erin: Images of a Global Ireland* (New Island Books, Dublin, 1996), pp. 46–52; Tony O'Reilly writing in *Sunday Independent*, 9 January 2000 and quoted in *Irish Times*, 2 November 1982.

47   Interview with Donal Donnelly, August 1999; *Challenge*, December 1967–December 1968; *National Land League Newsletter*, September 1971 and January 1972; *The Countryman: Organ of the National Land League*, 1973–4; *The National Land League: Its Origins, Aims, Structures and Disciplines*, n.d. (thanks to Donal Donnelly).

48   *Irish Times*, 3 June 1969; Conor Cruise O'Brien, *Memoir: My Life and Themes* (Profile Books, London, 1998), pp. 326–34.

49   McInerney, p. 243.

50   Brendan O hEithir writing in *Hibernia*, 2 January 1976; Benedict Kiely writing in *Irish Times*, 28 September 1985; James Plunkett, review from the O'Brien Press, courtesy of Peter Hegarty, n.d.; Gonzalez, p. 67.

51   *Irish Times*, 2 November 1982 and 19–26 August 1985; *Monkeys*, pp. i–ii.

52   O'Donnell interview with J.P. McHugh, 1979, cited in McHugh, 'Voices', p. 218; Foreword, *Not Yet Emmet – A Wreath on the Grave of Sean Murray* (New Books, Dublin, n.d. [1985]); *Irish Times*, *Irish Press* and *Irish Independent*, 14–17 May 1986.

Conclusion

1 Dunphy, p. 188.
2 Irish Communist Organisation, *The Irish Republican Congress* (ICO, London, 1966), p. 39.
3 Peadar O'Donnell, Foreword to George Gilmore, *Labour and the Republican Movement* (Republican Publications, Dublin, 1966).
4 *AP*, 1 August 1931.
5 *Irish Press*, 10 January 1983.
6 *Monkeys*, p. 30.
7 *Irish Times*, 1 March 1963.
8 Francis Doherty, 'Windows on the World', *Fortnight*, December 1990; Gonzalez, pp. 7, 12 and 120; Terry Eagleton, *Crazy John and the Bishop and Other Essays in Irish Culture* (Cork University Press, Cork, 1998), p. 239.
9 *This Week in Ireland*, vol. 1, no. 20, 27 February, 1970.
10 Michael D. Higgins, 'Liam O'Flaherty and Peadar O'Donnell – Images of Rural Community', *The Crane Bag*, vol. 9, no. 1, 1985, p. 41.
11 See Philip O'Leary, 'The Donegal of Seamus Ó Grianna and Peadar O'Donnell, *Éire-Ireland*, vol. 23, no. 2, 1988.
12 *Salud!*, p. 22; 'At the Sign of the Donkey Cart', *The Bell*, vol. 12, no. 2, May 1946, p. 96.
13 McInerney, p. 197; *AP*, 25 June 1932; *Studies*, xlvii, 1958, pp. 31–3.
14 McInerney, p. 197.
15 *Irish Times*, 22 February 1983.
16 Ibid.
17 *AP*, 17 September 1927.
18 *AP*, 7 February 1931.
19 McDyer, p. 83.
20 Richard English, 'Green on Red: Two Case Studies in Early Twentieth Century Irish Republican Thought', D.G. Boyce, Robert Eccleshall and Vincent Geoghan (eds), *Political Thought in Ireland Since the Seventeenth Century* (Routledge, London and New York), p. 175.
21 Grattan Freyer, 'Peadar O'Donnell: Novelist and Revolutionary', *Ireland Guide* (Bord Fáilte, Dublin, 1982), p. 36.
22 See, for example, English, *Radicals and the Republic, passim.*; interviews with former IRA activists in Mac Eoin, *Twilight Years*; *Irish Socialist*, June 1986; Eamon McCann writing in *Sunday Tribune*, 19 December 1999; Jim Kemmy, reported in *Irish Times*, 22 August 1985.

Guide to further reading

There have been three previous biographical treatments of Peadar O'Donnell: Grattan Freyer, *Peadar O'Donnell* (Bucknell University Press, Lewisburg, 1973); Michael McInerney, *Peadar O'Donnell: Irish Social Rebel* (The O'Brien Press, Dublin, 1974), and Peter Hegarty, *Peadar O'Donnell* (Mercier Press, Cork, 1999). Freyer's short book was part of a series on Irish writers and is primarily an introduction to O'Donnell's literature. McInerney's book is less a biography than a sympathetic, extended political profile based on interviews with O'Donnell. Hegarty's recent publication is the first biography worthy of the name. Written in popular, accessible style, it is particularly strong on O'Donnell's family and social background, his early years, and his war of independence experiences. Hegarty's primary concern is with giving us a picture of O'Donnell 'the man', rather than with an analysis of his politics.

O'Donnell himself wrote three autobiographical accounts: *The Gates Flew Open* (Jonathan Cape, London, 1932), *Salud! An Irishman in Spain* (Methuen, London, 1937) and *There Will Be Another Day* (Dolmen Press, Dublin, 1963). These deal respectively with his years in prison from 1922 to 1924, his time in Spain at the beginning of the civil war in 1936, and the period of the land annuities agitation, 1926–32. *Monkeys in the Superstructure: Reminiscences of Peadar O'Donnell* (Salmon Press, Galway, 1986) is the text of a speech he delivered in 1985 in which he looks back episodically over his political life. His seven novels and one play (see text and references) are all essential reading for anyone with an interest in deepening their understanding of O'Donnell. His published political pamphlets are: *Plan of Campaign for Irish Working Farmers* (Fodhla, Dublin,

1931); *For or Against the Ranchers?* *Irish Working Farmers and the Economic War* (Mayo News, Westport, 1932); *The Bothy Fire and All That* (Irish People Publications, Dublin, 1937); *The Role of Industrial Workers in the Problems of the West* (*The Kerryman*, Tralee, n.d. [1966]) – originally published as *The Problem of the West* (Mayo News, Swinford, 1966); and *Not Yet Emmet – A Wreath on the Grave of Sean Murray* (New Books, Dublin, n.d. [1985]). The largest concentrations of his writings on political, social and cultural affairs are to be found in the pages of *An Phoblacht* (1926–33), *Republican Congress* (1934–5) and *The Bell* (1940–54).

O'Donnell's trade union years have been comprehensively covered by Anton McCabe in '"The Stormy Petrel of the Transport Workers": Peadar O'Donnell, Trade Unionist, 1917–1920', *Saothar*, 19, 1994. For general context on labour and politics in these years, see C. Desmond Greaves, *The Irish Transport and General Workers' Union: The Formative Years, 1909–1923* (Gill and Macmillan, Dublin, 1982) and *Liam Mellows and the Irish Revolution* (Lawrence and Wishart, London, 1971); Emmet O'Connor, *Syndicalism in Ireland, 1917–1923* (Cork University Press, Cork, 1988); Conor Kostick, *Revolution in Ireland: Popular Militancy, 1917 to 1923* (Pluto Press, London, 1996); Arthur Mitchell, *Labour in Irish Politics, 1890–1930* (Irish University Press, Dublin, 1974); and E. Rumpf and A.C. Hepburn, *Nationalism and Socialism in Twentieth Century Ireland* (Liverpool University Press, Liverpool, 1977). Dorothy MacArdle's classic republican chronicle of the War of Independence and Civil War years, *The Irish Republic* (Gollancz, London, 1937), remains invaluable, while Michael Hopkinson's *Green Against Green: The Irish Civil War* (Gill and Macmillan, Dublin, 1988) is the clearest available general account of that conflict. J. Bowyer Bell, *The Secret Army: The IRA* (Poolbeg, Dublin, 1989; first edn. 1970), Tim Pat Coogan, *The IRA* (Pall Mall, London, 1970) and Conor Foley, *Legion of the Rearguard: The IRA and the Modern Irish State* (Pluto Press, London, 1992) all cover the IRA in these and in the subsequent years of O'Donnell's involvement. Uinseann MacEoin's *Survivors* (Argenta, Dublin, 1980) and *The IRA in the Twilight Years, 1923–1948* (Argenta, Dublin, 1997) are other useful reference books for this period. O'Donnell features prominently in (and wrote a foreword to) Sean Cronin, *Frank Ryan: The Search for the Republic* (Repsol, Dublin, 1980).

The best available account and analysis of Irish communism in the twentieth century is Mike Milotte's *Communism in Modern Ireland: The Pursuit of the Workers' Republic since 1916* (Gill and Macmillan, Dublin, 1984), which, like Kostick's book, is a scholarly work written from a particular Trotskyist perspective. See also the CPI's potted history of itself, *Communist Party of Ireland: Outline History* (New Books, Dublin, n.d.). Useful articles on communism and republicanism in the 1920s and 1930s include Stephen Bowler, 'Sean Murray and the Pursuit of Stalinism in One Country', *Saothar* 18, 1993; Emmet O'Connor, 'Jim Larkin and the Communist Internationals, 1923–9', *Irish Historical Studies*, xxxi, 123, May 1999; Barry McLoughlin and Emmet O'Connor, 'Sources on Ireland and the Communist International', *Saothar* 21, 1996; and Jonathan Hammill, 'Saor Éire and the IRA: An Exercise in Deception?', *Saothar* 20, 1995. Essential reading also is James Hogan's polemical red-scare tract, *Could Ireland become Communist? The Facts of the Case* (Cahill, Dublin, 1935), which features O'Donnell as the leading bogey man.

Richard English has published a number of articles relating to O'Donnell and his political activities in the 1920s and 1930s; most of his research findings and (hostile and negative) judgements are gathered in his book *Radicals and the Republic: Socialist Republicanism in the Irish Free State 1925–1937* (Clarendon Press, Oxford, 1994). For English, O'Donnell is representative of what he sees as the intellectual shortcomings of interwar socialist republicanism. Prior to English, Henry Patterson in *The Politics of Illusion: Republicanism and Socialism in Modern Ireland* (Hutchinson Radius, London, 1989) (reissued as *The Politics of Illusion: A Political History of the IRA* (Serif, London, 1997))had offered the most detailed critique of O'Donnell as the personification of what he terms 'social republicanism'. They both stress what they see as the incompatibility of militant nationalism and socialism and use the political success of Fianna Fáil to highlight the failures of the republican left. Richard Dunphy shares the neo-Marxist approach of Patterson in his very useful *The Making of Fianna Fáil Power in Ireland 1923–1948* (Clarendon Press, Oxford, 1995), and a similar note is struck in Paul Bew, Ellen Hazelkorn and Henry Patterson, *The Dynamics of Irish Politics* (Lawrence and Wishart, London, 1989). A welcome addition to the historiography of politics in interwar Ireland is Fearghal McGarry's *Irish Politics and the Spanish Civil War* (Cork University Press, Cork, 1999). Two participant accounts of the Republican Congress from comrades of O'Donnell's are George Gilmore, *The Irish Republican Congress* (Cork Workers' Club, Cork, 1978 edn) and Patrick Byrne, *The Irish Republican Congress Revisited* (Connolly Association, London, 1994 edn).

On O'Donnell's fiction, see Alexander Gonzalez, *Peadar O'Donnell: A Readers' Guide* (Dufour Editions, Chester Springs, 1997); Philip O'Leary, 'The Donegal of Seamus Ó Grianna and Peadar O'Donnell', *Éire-Ireland*, vol. 23, no. 2, Summer 1988; Michael D. Higgins, 'Liam O'Flaherty and Peadar O'Donnell – Images of Rural Community', *The Crane Bag*, vol. 9, no. 1, 1985; Richard English, '"Scenes that surround certain conflicts": The literature of Peadar O'Donnell reconsidered', in Eve Patten (ed.), *Returning to Ourselves* (Lagan Press, Belfast, 1995); and Francis Doherty, 'Windows on the world', *Fortnight*, December 1990. The latter also contains a warm profile of O'Donnell, 'Evangelical Puritanism', by Owen Dudley Edwards.

Index